Walt F.J. Goodridge, author of *Turn Your Passion Into Profit* • *Living True to Your Self* • *Ducks in a Row (How to find the courage to finally QUIT your soul-draining, life- sapping, energy-depleting, freedom-robbing job now... before it's too late...and live passionately ever after!)* and star of the "Jamaican in China" travel blog, presents the next stage in your evolution: the untethered lifestyle!

A pocket guide of income strategies, travel jobs & survival tips for expats, vagabonds, techies and rat race escapees who want to see the world AND make money too!
by Walt F.J. Goodridge

How to Become a Nomadpreneur:
A Pocket Guide of Income Strategies, Travel Jobs & Survival Tips for Expats, Vagabonds, Techies and Rat Race Escapees Who Want To See the World and Make Money Too!
© Walt F.J. Goodridge. All rights reserved.

This book may not be reproduced in whole or in part, or transmitted in any form, without written permission from the author and publisher, except by a reviewer who may quote brief passages in a review. Contact: walt@waltgoodridge.com

Published by Walt F.J. Goodridge
dba a company called W
ISBN: 978-1539170365 (AMAZ)

Visit a store called W

Books, apps, audio, video, merchandise, courses, Walt's passion projects, freebies and more from a company called W
www.waltgoodridge.com/store

Distributed by
The Passion Profit Company

Educational institutions, government agencies, libraries and corporations are invited to inquire about quantity discounts.
(646) 481-4238 | sales@passionprofit.com

Paperback rinted in the United States of America

Table of Contents

Dedication 4
Acknowledgments 4

SECTION I: MINDSET

Preliminaries 5
Prologue 9
1 Freedom 13
2 Defined 23
3 Required 27

SECTION II: MONEY
4 Method 51
5 Strategies 57
6 Jobs 77
7 Secrets 91

SECTION III: MOBILITY
8 Motivation 105
9 Logistics 111
10 Resources 121

SECTION IV: MORE

Appendix 136
About the Author 142
Free Resources for the Nomadpreneur 144
Books from the Passionpreneur Series 145
Books from the Hip Hop Entrepreneur Series 146
Resources from the Ageless Adept Series 147
Books from the Ageless Adept Series 148
All the Channels & Blogs 149
Tests & Quizzes 150

Dedication [toc]

This book is dedicated to my
grandmother, Isolene Rebecca Golding
ever since - 1907-1988 - evermore

Acknowledgments [toc]

I wish to thank Thelma Goodridge and Nyembane Goodridge for making me who I am, and also Reina Joa, Christine Karmo, Randy Hyde, Pramod Khanna, Ken McRae, Ernest Capers, Dr. Heru Shango, Zelda Samara Owens, Nicole Drew, Diamond Davis, Tony Cordoza, Monica Afesi, Stacey Spencer-Willoughby, Howard Walters, Aaron Willoughby, Wayne Wright, Gurdeep Singh, Delxino Wilson de Briano, Joe Hill, Catherine Young, Ashley Moffatt, Jayvee Vallejera, Chun Yu Wang, Ron McFarlane, and Preeyaporn Jompeang, who have all helped me act from, create, demonstrate and live true to my belief system.

SECTION I: MINDSET ▲
Preliminaries [toc]

Who
Work at home. Wander and roam.

As the book's subtitle indicates, this information is for passionpreneurs, infopreneurs, vagabondpreneurs, restless techies, expats, fugitive escapees from corporate cubicle confinement, and anyone who simply wants the freedom to create an untethered lifestyle based on an income strategy that doesn't require one's presence!

Why

I wrote this guide because people asked me to:

> *Hey Walt, You're actually living the life I've always wanted...to be anywhere in the world with my computer and still be making money. So tell me, how are you able to travel around from country to country? How do you work your business?*—**Roy**

Someone asked again during one of my passionpreneur teleclasses:

> *Walt, I want to make a break for it and live in another country, but I have mortgages to pay. My fantasy life would be to be a full time writer, traveling internationally and writing novels, historical essays and getting paid to speak about it.*—**Teleclass participant**

I realized people were asking for a template; a guide book for how things work behind the scenes! Therefore, I decided to share the nuts and bolts— the actual strategies, tools and software I use to make money, maintain mobility, survive and run multiple identities as a nomadpreneur. This is my private, top secret "Operations Manual for Freedom!"

I've divided the information into three sections:

Mindset

First, I'll cover the belief system and behaviors I believe are necessary to create *and sustain* the nomadpreneur lifestyle. This is the foundation.

Money

Next, I'll share the strategies, software, setup and customized system I use to make money, maintain mobility and survive as a nomadpreneur! You'll get just about everything I use to run my business except my user ids and passwords! I'll also share strategies others have used that you can use to create your own nomadpreneur lifestyle.

Mobility

Finally, I'll provide tips and advice for traveling the world at minimal cost and a step-by-step checklist for getting started.

Process

To get the most from this book, never continue reading past a word or phrase you don't understand! Use a dictionary or search online for the most appropriate meaning. This tip is more important than people realize! It's been shown that the only reason people give up on a new project or course of study is that they encounter a word, phrase or concept for which they have no definition, or the wrong definition.

Use the check boxes (☐). After you've read and performed the necessary activity or are sure you understand its significance, place a check in the box, initial it, place the date next to it. Think of this as an agreement between you and your future self.

Read this guide at least twice—once for a general overview, and again to take notes and action!

Fulfill the pre-requisites. This guide is based in part on my Passion Profit™ Philosophy and Formula.

Read or listen to *Turn Your Passion Into Profit*

Take the Personality Test at passionprofit.com/itest2 to find your purpose

Read *Ducks in a Row: How to find the courage to finally QUIT your soul-draining, life-sapping, energy-depleting, freedom-robbing job now, before it's too late, and live passionately ever after*!

Profiles

Throughout this book, I'll share profiles of real individuals—some I know and others I've heard about—who are doing some form of nomadpreneuring. There are some who truly roam, while others have simply found a place they like and end up staying there for months or years. I include them all! No snobbery here! What I respect and wish to encourage is simply the boldness to jump into the unknown and carve out a life in a new location.

Point

All the information I share, including my fun adventures in China, are offered to make a point: to show that we can all make different choices; to show how it can be done, and thereby, encourage and empower others to do the same!

> *"I'm not here to convince, justify, defend or apologize for my beliefs, choices or lifestyle. I'm not here for validation, vindication or approval, nor to respond to personal attacks. I'm here to share a philosophy & formula that work for me and others. And in a world of over seven billion people, if one person can do a thing, then it must be possible for at least one other person to do the same. It is with this underlying belief that I share these ideas."*

Prologue [toc]

A prelude to action

This is a book about taking action. Let me rephrase that: *this is a book intended and designed to be used to take action.* It is not entertainment. It is not simply research. It is not theory, nor should it be seen as merely a journal of what I and others have been able to achieve. It is a book designed to empower you to take real, concrete action, in a real and concrete world with the goal of making *your* dreams real and concrete.

It's been my experience that people take action when it comes to things that are important to them. People *always* find time for things that matter to them.

I learned during sales classes for a network marketing company I was once a part of that people can be moved to the action of jumping into our business opportunity by (a) money, (b) fun, (c) information/knowledge and (d) the desire to help others. There are, of course, variations and nuance within those broad categories of motivations, but the point was that if we could speak the language of motivation that mattered to our potential prospect, we would have more success in our recruitment efforts.

My own motivation was freedom, which fell somewhere in between *money* and *fun*. While I didn't need truckloads of money to be happy, I *did* desire the freedom that an alternative source of income can often provide. I quit my job, escaped from America and became a nomadpreneur all in the pursuit of freedom—more on that later.

I suggest to you that in order for *you* to take the necessary action required to become a nomadpreneur, that you first gain clarity on your "why." Why are you reading this book? Why are you contemplating this lifestyle? Are you considering doing it for the money? Are you doing it for the fun and adventure? Are you running from something, or someone?

Fear can be a powerful motivator. While I don't suggest you live life in a constant state of fear, later I'll share how fear (or what I perceived to be fear) was at the basis of my own escape from the rat race.

I refer to the lifestyle advocated in this book as "the next stage in an evolution." Nomadpreneuring is not a lifestyle many people can simply step into after years of being trained as an employee. In order to become a nomadpreneur, it may be necessary for you to rethink what it means to be gainfully employed; to reevaluate what it means to have a job, to be successful, to be sensible, practical and all the traits you've been led to believe are admirable and desirable. It may be necessary to go **in search of a better belief system** about things you believe in and thought were inviolate.

Once you realize there is a better way to live your life, you may decide it's time to get serious about living true to your self.

It may be necessary to discover what your grand purpose in life really is and to honor your passion.
You may feel empowered with the realization that:
Your PASSION is part of your life's purpose
EVERYONE has a passion
ALL passions have value
ANY passion can be turned into profit, and that
You can make money doing what you love!

With your belief level raised, it may be necessary to spend time developing that passion creating a product to **turn your passion into profit** because you realize:

"The only way to take control of your life, raise your standard of living and move beyond merely surviving is to create your own unique product or service that you offer to increasing numbers of people in exchange for the things of value you desire. This simple formula applies to countries as well as people. A self-sufficient economy has its own products or services of value to export to the world. Similarly, a self-sufficient individual has something of value to exchange in the global marketplace. That thing of value is best based on your natural talent, skill, or interest—in other words, your passion!"

You may need to overcome your belief that others are better, wealthier or more connected than you, or that your ideas are not marketable. You may need to practice acting with confidence and positive expectations based on the assurance that:

"If you create and market a product or service through a business that is in alignment with your personality, capitalizes on your history, incorporates your experiences, harnesses your talents, optimizes your strengths, complements your weaknesses, honors your life's purpose, and moves you towards the conquest of your own fears, there is ABSOLUTELY NO WAY that anyone in this or any other universe can offer the same value that you do!"

Even if you achieve success turning that passion into profit, you may still be tethered to a job you desperately desire to quit, and realize that no amount of preparation seems enough to get your **ducks in a row** and that something else is required to show you **how to find the courage to finally quit your soul- draining, life-sapping, energy-depleting, freedom- robbing job now...before it's too late...and live passionately ever after!**

Perhaps this has been your journey. Or, perhaps you simply woke up ready to take a courageous leap into this lifestyle. However you arrived here, I hope to offer you that elusive "something else" to help you untether yourself and achieve your dream! Read on!

CHAPTER 1: Freedom [toc]

Putting the "mad" in nomad!

Once upon a time

It was just one of those seemingly spontaneous, but subconsciously orchestrated decisions, stemming from a set of seemingly random, but divinely engineered sequence of events, that led to my seemingly serendipitous, but cosmically inevitable arrival on the remote Pacific island of Saipan to live my dream life.

My name is Walt F.J. Goodridge, author of *Turn Your Passion Into Profit* and *Living True to Your Self*, and star of the "Jamaican in China" blog. I am a nomadpreneur. From my base on a tropical island in the Pacific, I now have the freedom to travel the world *and* generate money through online and offline income strategies. It wasn't always like this, however. Let me share with you how it all started.

It was December, and my friend, Ken M., who lived in Las Vegas, Nevada, USA at the time, happened to be in Brooklyn, New York, visiting a friend. He invited me to a holiday party that was to take place on Saturday, December 17.

That Saturday, I made the long, late night train ride from Harlem, in uptown Manhattan—where I lived at the time—to the neighboring borough of Brooklyn.

The party ended at about 3:00 a.m. or 4:00 a.m. Sunday morning, and as I prepared to leave, Ken offered to drive me back home. We discovered, however, that Ken's car was blocked in the driveway by a neighbor's car that was parked on the street. Ken suggested we knock on the neighbor's door to request that she let us out. I suggested, however, rather than wake the neighbor so early on a Sunday morning, that we simply wait it out, and take the opportunity to chat and catch up on our lives as we hadn't had time to do so amid the noise of the party. The neighbor would likely be up in a few hours to go to church anyway.

After touching on a few random topics, Ken and I got into a discussion about his recent trip to Japan to produce some music for some Japanese recording artists. While there, the musicians took Ken and his co-producer to the island of Saipan, Northern Mariana Islands, to work with another producer on that island.

Ken and his co-producer had such a wonderful time on Saipan that they returned several months later for another round. As he revealed the details of his "good time" to me that night in Brooklyn, something about his adventure piqued my interest, sparked my curiosity, and stirred a latent nomadic streak that had been submerged for all these years.

The prospect of living my life in a whole new world came at a time when, jaded by the materialism and crowded yet paradoxically isolated living of big city life, I was seeking to reinvent myself.

Ken's pitch contained all the right words and phrases: warm weather, beautiful people (read: women), slower lifestyle, all while on the U.S. postal system—an important consideration for my mail order business. Yes, something clicked, and I made a decision that very night that I was Saipan-bound!

Freedom Song

Over the next several weeks, I prepared to make the transition. Ken introduced me to a long-time resident of Saipan, and we talked briefly by phone. I started researching Saipan and the region, made connections on couchsurfing.org, and booked my flights for the journey. As the fateful day of my departure approached, I sent the following email to a few friends, family, customers and clients:

February 9

hi all, As you may have surmised, and as I've hinted at in several of my recent Friday Life Rhymes* (specifically #437 entitled "Freedom Song"), something's been brewing in "Walt World" for the past few months.

Ever since leaving corporate America a few years ago, I've been executing a plan to create the lifestyle of a modern, minimalist, nomadic, passionpreneur based on a passive-residual income stream! In other words, I want out of the rat race!

Now that I've cut all the tethers and structured a turnkey, self-sustaining, internet-based business that doesn't require my physical presence in any one location...drum roll, please....

...I've bought a one way ticket to the island of Saipan in the South Pacific! [Saipan is actually in the Western Pacific, but South sounded so much more exotic]

So amid sea, sand and sun, I'll be living my dream in a clime that resonates with who I wish to be.

Since this is simply the first step in a journey of a thousand smiles, I didn't want to make a big deal about it until I got there and surveyed the lay of the land. But, I wanted to tell a few friends and contacts who I felt deserve a little advanced notice...

You can still reach me at walt@passionprofit.com, and I'll set up a Skype™ account for anyone who'd like to keep in touch, and share the experience with me! — Walt

p.s. I leave next Wed February 15 for Las Vegas, and then I'm on to Japan—my first stop on the way to Saipan! If you know of anyone there in Tokyo I can call who might be able to show me around, please let me know. And in case you didn't receive Life Rhyme* #437, here it is again:

Freedom Song

One day you'll think about me:
Haven't seen him in a while
You'll make a note to find me
or a number you can dial

One day you'll ask about me:
Where on earth can he be found?
And learn at last I've set my sail
where sun and sea abound

One day you'll say about me:
Goes the nomad on his way
To live the life's adventure
that he said he would some day

One day you'll write about me:
There's a man who lived his dream
Cut loose the oars and left the boat
to swim a different stream

And then one day amid the noise
and hustle of the throng
You'll hear a tune first faintly
that's been playing all along

You'll know the singer instantly
you'll recognize my voice
A heart-felt freedom song
of life lived not by chance but choice... [end of email]

*Walt's Life Rhymes: a weekly inspirational email I sent for 9 years to 10,000 subscribers. Archives at liferhymes.com

Not mad, nomad!

It was very empowering and satisfying to be able to write and send that "Freedom Song" email and to actually embark on the journey of a lifetime. Yes, some people thought I was mad, as in crazy! But, I wasn't going mad, I was going nomad!

I bought my airline ticket, gave away my 2500-strong vinyl LP collection, donated my books to a combination of friends and street vendors, unloaded almost everything I owned, and two months after that fateful conversation in Brooklyn, and a week after that "Freedom Song" email, I executed my escape from America, and touched down on the island of Saipan exactly sixty-eight days after first hearing of it!

I always think about the fact that had I not gone to that party that night, and had Ken and I not opted to wait out the wee morning hours engaged in conversation, the topic of travel and Saipan may not ever have come up presenting an option for this now quite happy nomadpreneur. What mightn't have been.

Impetus
*"This is exactly what I worked 40
years so I could do!"*
—retiree traveler

I once read an article about a group of travelers on a tour of the Galapagos Islands in the Eastern Pacific. For many of them, it was the adventure of a lifetime.

One of the travelers—an approximately 72 year old male—was quoted as saying: "You know what? This is exactly what I worked 40 years so I could do!"

Of course, I felt happy for him that he was doing something he'd always wanted to do. At the same time, however, the statement struck me as one of the saddest I'd ever heard. Let me explain why.

You see, at the beginning of their careers, many people plan their lives according to the "40-40-40 plan." That's the life plan where you work 40 hours per week, for 40 years of your life, and retire with a pension of 40% of your income.

When I started my first job in corporate America, that plan was the basis of conversation and actual planning I heard several of the other new engineers engaged in on their first day of work! It scared me.

"I'm just an average guy who decided he couldn't wait 40 years for his freedom." —me

That's when the fire was first lit. I decided right then and there—within the first fifteen minutes of my first job straight out of college—that I would become a nomadpreneur. Actually, I hadn't yet coined that word. What I actually decided was that I needed to escape, and vowed to create a lifestyle of freedom.

To make a long story short: that's what I did.

Seven years later, I walked away from that civil engineering job to pursue my passion. For years afterwards, I crafted what turned out to be the perfect business foundation for the nomadpreneur lifestyle. So, when the opportunity to execute came to me on that night in Brooklyn, I was ready.

As a result, I'm no longer limited to experiencing the wider world in two-week vacations every twelve months as I did when I was an employee, or after forty years of working like that Galapagos traveler. If I want to travel from Saipan to Jamaica for two weeks, and then spend a few months in New York, and then head over to China, I can do that (and I have). There's no physical location I have to return to in order to resume generating income. My streams of income are independent of where I am physically located.

NEXT: Mastering the "one-hour work day!"

Mastering the "one-hour work day!"

Since my escape, I've spent the last several years further tweaking and nomadizing my lifestyle. That has included embracing minimalism, reducing my "per diem footprint," putting my business on "autopilot," establishing a template and system for creating books and audio products, streamlining web hosting, bill payment, delivery of my products, and also streamlining the business monitoring and customer service processes so that all I need is a wi-fi hotspot to check my emails, visitor stats and sales in less than an hour every day or every few days if I simply want to untether for longer periods. As a result, I can spend the rest of my time doing what I love: writing, traveling and focusing on living a healthy, vegan lifestyle.

How's that been working for me? Well, I recently tested the system with a six-month adventure in China, Laos, Philippines and Singapore and wrote about it on the Jamaican in China blog (and in *Jamaican in China: Guess Who's Coming to Dim Sum*, Amazon).

***

Nomadpreneur Profile: Jamaican Jetsetter

Once upon a time, there was a Jamaican civil engineer living in New York who hated his job. He followed his passion, started a sideline business, escaped the rat race, ran off to a tropical island in the Pacific, and started a tourism business so he could give tours of the island to pretty girls every day...and live a nomadpreneur's dream life.

***

That's *my* story and I'm sticking to it! Hopefully, that story as well as the information in this book will inspire you to do something equally satisfying and fulfilling to honor your own dreams! Let's start filling in the details of *your* story, first with a few basics!

CHAPTER 2: Defined [toc|]

Credo, etymology, origin, history, types and you

"The flow of money into my life is not a function of an employer's largess or even local economic conditions. It is a function of my ability to recognize, create, communicate and exchange value with others worldwide. Therefore, I can generate money wherever in the world I am because I carry that ability with me wherever I go. I am a nomadpreneur!"—**The Nomadpreneur's Credo**

largess - *n.* generosity in bestowing money or gifts upon others

Definitions

NOMADPRENEUR: portmanteau of "nomad" and "entrepreneur"; one whose income strategy allows the freedom to travel while making money regardless of physical location.

nomad - *n.* 1550s, from Middle French nomade (16c.), from Latin Nomas (genitive Nomadis) "wandering groups in Arabia," from Greek nomas (genitive nomados, plural nomades) "roaming, roving, wandering" (to find pastures for flocks or herds)

entrepreneur - *n.* 1828, "manager or promoter of a theatrical production," reborrowing of Fr. entrepreneur "one who undertakes or manages," Old Fr. entreprendre "undertake." "Business manager" is from 1852.

portmanteau - *n.* a combination of 2 or more words or morphemes into one new word. *Maybe define morpheme, too?*

morpheme - *n.* a meaningful linguistic unit (a word/word element) that cannot be divided into smaller meaningful parts.

An extremely brief history of nomadpreneuring

Lest you think that nomadpreneuring is something new, let me assure you: Nomadpreneurs have existed ever since! Groups of prehistoric nomads met and traded with each other in the vast expanses of untamed continents. The traveling salesman of a bygone era was a nomadpreneur. The circus owner of yore made his money entertaining families in new locations every few weeks. Silk traders moved from one location to another in search of new markets. Yes, nomadpreneurs have always been with us. End of history lesson.

Types

However, what these classic nomadic entrepreneurs had in common is that the income streams they generated were dependent on the people in each new location. Once a trader left city A, she could only earn more money by finding a new city B. Her income stream from city A stopped flowing the moment she departed. That type of nomadpreneuring is what I refer to as location-specific, or **location-bound**.

As a modern, technology-enabled nomadpreneur, you now have the freedom to roam just like the traveling salesman, or circus owner, and tour like the musician, but with a difference: your income stream can be independent of what happens in each new location. In other words, you can move from city A, to city B to country C, and still earn money from any of those locations--or none of them--even while you're in continent D. Nomadpreneuring has become un- tethered. That type of nomadpreneuring is what I refer to as location-independent, or **location-free**.

What's the difference between a vagabond, a digital nomad and a nomadpreneur?
Answer: Well, besides the obvious answer (that I own the NOMADPRENUR.COM domain, not VAGABOND.COM or DIGITALNOMAD.COM!), there is overlap, of course, but vagabonding and digital nomading both have a temporary aesthetic to them. Both are vacation-like departures from a regular lifestyle to which one returns after the freedom ends. Since the foundation of the nomadpreneur lifestyle is the income strategy, a nomadpreneur always has that freedom.

Plan

In order to optimize your nomadpreneurial options, this book will give you strategies for creating location- bound *as well as* location-free income.

Caveats

I must share a few caveats before we continue:
• Nomadpreneuring need not be a "lifestyle for life." There's no standard that says you must nomadpreneur

forever. You can choose to nomadpreneur for a year or ten, then choose another lifestyle.

• If you're not prepared to live life a little on the edge or with a bit of uncertainty about outcomes, this may not be the right lifestyle for you.

• I can't guarantee it will be easy. In fact, nomadpreneuring may be the hardest thing to do.

• Nor can I guarantee your success. Surely you've heard stories of two people--children in the same household perhaps--given the same education, opportunity and tools, who produce dramatically different outcomes in life; one becomes a societal success, the other a crook!

In other words, I have no idea if you've arrived at this moment in time with the right mindset, life experience, motivation, discipline, creativity, persistence, astrological chart, life theme, soul age, personality or pre-ordained destiny to achieve success. What I *do* feel confident saying is that if you have the right combination of factors, and if something I share causes an epiphany in your self-concept and raises your belief level just enough, nothing can stop you!

Yes, my message is one of potential and possibilities! So, let's explore what you will need in order to optimize that potential and those possibilities.

CHAPTER 3: Required [toc]

What will it take to become a nomadpreneur?

Required: courage and discipline

"So, tell me. How did you have the confidence to go to China, without having a complete understanding of the language, a stable income stream, a job to back you up, and without the resources like friends, family and networks?"—**Tim**

That's the question Tim asked me at a recent holiday party. Tim is the father of six who lives in New Jersey. Though we communicate occasionally by email, we haven't seen each other that often since my escape from America. Whenever we do see each other, however, he refers to me as "My Hero!" It was too noisy at the party for me to go into the depth of answer I wanted to, so we talked by phone a few days later, and this is essentially what I shared with him:

Confidence?

It is my belief and experience—and an underlying truth I share in all my books—that you can achieve just about anything you desire in life if you have two things: courage and discipline.

> *"Courage is discipline in the face of fear.*
> *Discipline is courage in the face of distraction."*

Once you are introduced to the possibility of a new reality (that you can make money as a nomadpreneur, for instance) with a different belief system, a different set of choices, required actions, consequences and benefits, it requires COURAGE to choose to embark on that reality in the face of fear and habit.

Additionally, once you have actually embarked on the new path, it requires DISCIPLINE to maintain and sustain those actions in the face of doubt, derision, distraction and even downright sabotage.

You must first have the courage to pursue the thing you believe in, and then the discipline to keep doing so. Make no mistake: It takes courage and discipline to make money doing what you love. It takes courage and discipline to become a nomadpreneur.

Many people—authors, gurus, manufacturers—will try to sell you on quick and easy strategies for everything from losing weight to making money to having a better sex life. They will offer you a magic pill or fairy dust that promises to work like a charm— partly because that's what people have been conditioned to want. However, there is often something missing from these formulas.

If their products do, in fact, legitimately offer the success they purport to, what they fail to mention, and what ultimately dooms the hopeful buyer to failure is the seller's glaring omission of the words *"courage and discipline not included"*. That's what all success boils down to. It doesn't matter whether the goal is losing weight, or finding true love, courage and discipline are the complementary and inextricably linked sides of every coin of success. Any solution that suggests otherwise is doing you a disservice.

To create and sustain a nomadpreneur lifestyle, you need the courage to:
- believe something new about yourself.
- believe something new about how to make money.
- take the steps to board the plane, train, bus or car.
- Then you need the discipline to:
- keep assessing and tweaking your strategies.
- keep trying new strategies.

What Tim referred to as "confidence," I prefer to think of as a combination of courage and discipline. The courage to start. The discipline to continue. That, in my opinion, is what it required for me to become a nomadpreneur. Unfortunately, that part can't be taught. However, the good news is you *can* develop those traits regardless of the internal and external challenges you believe you face. First, though, you need to find those traits within yourself. Where do you go looking for them? Where do courage and discipline come from? Who can say? Everyone is different. Perhaps it comes from formative childhood experiences or transformative life challenges and training from a mentor. Perhaps it's in your DNA. Perhaps it's in your "chart." Perhaps it's an ingrained part of your life theme or soul age or personality type. I'm not sure I can tell you where to go looking. It's something you'll have to discover and nurture on your own.

In my own life, there have definitely been some transformative life experiences that prepared me for becoming a nomadpreneur. After going through three evictions, sleeping on friends' couches and pawning my possessions to survive during my early life as a passionpreneur, I developed the awareness that everything is survivable. After coming home to find an eviction notice on my apartment door, then allowing the process to play out to see what awaited on the other side, a lot of life's seemingly "major" challenges that would cripple or paralyze others (or a previous version of myself) became minor in comparison. If I could survive being homeless in New York, I can survive being a nomad in China!

Consequently, all the potential challenges of nomadpreneuring—unfamiliar language and culture, unstable income, lack of support—are all survivable with the courage and discipline my experiences have honed within me.

Required: live true to your self

"To be yourself in a world that is constantly trying to make you something else is the greatest accomplishment." — Ralph Waldo Emerson

Having the right motivation is a requirement.

For me, that fateful, first fifteen minute glimpse of what corporate life would be like was all the motivation I needed to create a different life for myself. I was so fearful of living a life of servitude and entrapment, that nothing was going to stop me.

Finding the "courage" to quit my job and jump out on my own may *seem* like a bold move, but once I realized that without some kind of action I would be condemning myself to the soul-draining, life-sapping, energy-depleting, freedom-robbing life I was on track to suffer through, escape became a no-brainer! Similarly, jumping on a plane to escape from America to live on Saipan, or traveling to China to live for six months may seem like bold, radical risks, but that's only if you're not inside my head with my thoughts and belief system.

If you believed the things I believe, feared the things I fear, and valued the things I value, then such moves are the only logical, emotional and practical steps to take. I call that *living true to my self.*

Many believe they are living true to themselves.

Here is my test from *Living True to Your Self*:
- Have you identified your purpose in life?
- Are you in control of how you spend your time?
- Are you engaged in activities that fulfill your purpose?
- Are you in employment* that contradicts your values?
- Are you in relationships* that contradict your ethics?
- Are you living in the location and lifestyle of your bliss?

(Are you buying, selling, making, marketing or otherwise endorsing the buying, selling, making or marketing of goods and services or involved in lifestyles or relationships that are at odds with your values or ethics simply for a paycheck?)

In the broadest terms, living true to your self means, as a friend of mine was fond of saying, "displaying the appropriate and healthy level of self-advocacy." In other words, I, as my own advocate, must strive at all times to think, speak, be and behave in ways that support my physical, mental and spiritual survival, growth, and prosperity without infringing on the same of others and without compromising my ethics and values. It means being in control of and steering my life towards the fulfillment of my purpose. It means engaging in a profession that serves that purpose. It means getting out of unhealthy relationships even if children are involved. It means living where and how I wish to live.

How do you get there? This mindset of living true to my self spans a wide range of beliefs including: how I perceive myself; what I believe is possible in life; what I believe is possible for me; how I perceive *and honor* my purpose in life; how I deal with what others interpret as setbacks, etc... Some of those mindset

beliefs include:
- I can create the life I desire.
- Every goal is achievable.
- Every destination is a series of steps from A to Z.
- There is a way, a path I can take to get there.
- If others have done it, I can do it too.

Living Truism: In order to live true to your self, you must be in control of your life.

Yes, being a nomadpreneur is one way to *live true to your self*!

***

Nomadpreneur Profile

Heru makes herbal juices and does health consulting. He got tired of living in the Bronx. So, he jetted to the US Virgin Islands. Now he grows his own herbs, sells juices and consults from his new home in the tropics!

***

Required: recognize the insanity

"You'll never be able to truly escape the rat race unless you can see it objectively for what it is. It is an unnatural and abnormal construct."

It's been said that the first step in making meaningful change is awareness. In other words, you must be fully aware of your situation before you can take the necessary steps to change it. The challenge, as I see it, is that people have taken what is a very insane, abnormal, unnatural, unsustainable situation and made it seem sane, normal, natural and sustainable. You and I are living in a bizarre nightmare, but because everyone else is here with us, and because no one is screaming in terror at the predicament, we, too, have accepted it as normal.

You've obviously felt there was something unfulfilling about this paradigm we're living in, or else you wouldn't be reading this book. However, I'm going to do you a favor. I'm going to show you just how deep the rabbit hole goes in an effort to offer you some real motivation for escape. Unless and until you truly see things as they are, it will always be a challenge for you to escape.

You'll never be able to truly escape the rat race unless you can see it objectively for what it is. It is an unnatural, abnormal construct.

Think about this. If you lived in a natural environment, there would be two things you needed to survive—only two basic freedoms of real value: a place to exist, and time to do as you please.

A "place to exist" means a place that you own free and clear and that does not require payment of any kind in order for you to exist on it. You are not free if you have to pay someone for a place to exist.

The "time to do as you please" means the time to devote to any exercise or endeavor you choose without interference, obligation or contract. You are not free if someone else is in control of your time.

So, let me say again: without a place to call your own on which you can create and cultivate the means for your survival (i.e., land), you are never truly free. Additionally, without control of your time to do the things you desire, you are never truly free.

That is all you need in order to be free, survive, and prosper: a place to call your own, and the time to do as you please. (This supposes, of course, that at least some of that land and/or at least some of your time is devoted to creating sustenance in the form of food to eat, and shelter in the form of protection from the elements as required.)

Now, as much as you have been led to believe otherwise, everything else you have been told is necessary for your happiness and freedom, is contrived. Cell phones, cars, refrigerators, stereos, beds and televisions are not necessary for survival, happiness, peace of mind, contentment or true prosperity. Yes, they provide what we think of as convenience and comfort in the existing paradigm, but ultimately, they are not necessary for happiness and prosperity in the larger scheme of things.

Everything else beyond the basics is a construct. Everything is make believe. Everything else is optional. It is not part of the natural world.

Why is this important? Well, once you separate from the natural world to live in an unnatural world as we have, you must do unnatural things to maintain and sustain it. Once you move beyond life's basic concerns and freedoms; buy into the money construct upon which our unnatural construct is based, you must, by default and design, do unnatural things to sustain it.

Every every object, every activity, every endeavor we now accept as natural and normal is part and parcel of an unnatural design. To the degree that you buy into this unnaturalness, to that degree are you trapped within it and forced to do unnatural things to sustain it. It is unnatural to rise in opposition to your body's natural cycles and rhythms (before you're done sleeping) every day, day after day for a lifetime.

It is unnatural to travel underground in steel tubes with poor ventilation in unnaturally close proximity sharing surfaces and stale air with unhealthy people.

It is unnatural to spend a third of your life behind

a desk, in front of a computer, locked in a building, under artificial fluorescent light, away from fresh air and sunshine for eight or more hours each day.

It is unnatural as well as unhealthy to do shockingly repetitive tasks day after day subjecting your body and mind to physically and mentally numbing activities.

It is unnatural to drink stimulants each day to stay awake, or eat processed food every day for sustenance. I could go on. The bizarre truth is that every one of those conditions and activities I've just described could be considered a form of incarceration or even torture if used against our enemies during wartime.

It is insane to allow yourself to be subjected to this for an imaginary piece of paper with randomly assigned and arbitrary values in order to purchase entirely unnecessary and completely optional objects we've been told will make us happier or better people.

You are not insane for wanting a different lifestyle. The fact that you consider all this something to escape may actually be the sanest thought you've ever had!

Required: redefine success

The construct as just described is an idea that has been accepted and adopted as normal, but it's not the natural order of things. It's just a decision we've made as a society—or more accurately, that a smaller group has made for the majority. Every distinct and separate society can decide to create and live according to a different set of constructs.

Similarly, when you talk about individual achievements of financial success within a society, there are many things we take to be normal, that are, in fact, not natural.

This thing we call financial success--this idea we call wealth--this aspiration we call prosperity is based on a construct that says, among other things: more is better, the earth is ours to rape and pillage, consumerism is the order of the day, we must keep getting richer and richer by any means necessary. This "infinite growth through greed" concept is an unnatural construct imposed on the masses, and on nature, by ways of thought that are not in alignment with the natural order of things. A society could just as easily choose to base civilization upon harmony, sustainability, and meeting (not exceeding) the needs of the people, as Gandhi famously said.

It's as if you were born into a group of lemmings running desperately away from or towards some unknown quantity, so as soon as you hit the ground, you've got to start running, too! But none of the baby lemmings ever stop, look up and ask, "Mommy, why are we running?"

That's just the way it is. It's the way it has been for many years. It's what you've got to do to survive, but wait. Why??? And what if I disagree? What if I think this is insanity? What if I want to get off this crazy treadmill?

There's an inherent insanity in all of this that sane people must detach from if they are to remain sane. Becoming wealthy is not the solution. Wealth and its attainment is a pursuit that affords some flexibility and options while you're still incarcerated. It's like being the inmate in prison with the cigarettes for sale. Money simply allows you to move to a nicer part of the prison. Now, there's nothing inherently wrong with pursuing money. If you're going to be incarcerated, heck, you may as well live well, right? My warning to you, however, is not to make the mistake of seeing the pursuit of money as the route to real freedom and happiness. Furthermore, if you make the pursuit of money your goal without appreciating the larger context within which you pursue it, you may actually dig yourself deeper into the bowels of the prison.

I'm going to suggest to you that one of the best ways to pursue money is to actually detach a bit from the prevailing rat race, the existing lemming marathon and carve out a different path for yourself. Quitting your job might be the best first step in that journey.

Now, some people will never be able to "get" what I've just attempted to describe. They see the world as it is, and are functionally or soul-age-wise incapable of stepping back far enough to see it dispassionately and objectively. I imagine those people will not be reading this book—not yet anyway.

Required: adopt a better belief system

"Any belief system that is based on fear, encourages weakness, sanctions intolerance, threatens vengeance, promotes passivity and requires you to relinquish your personal power is doing you a disservice."—In Search of a Better Belief System

The concept of employment—of working a job in the paradigm as it is defined—is based on a faulty belief system. Yes, employment [the way it is practiced] robs you of your power and birthright to true freedom by separating you from your natural self. Employment is a bitter belief system. Perhaps it's time to find one better. *[End of Excerpt]*

Quitting my job and escaping the rat race to live on a tropical island in the Pacific with the freedom to roam the Asia Pacific region was how I executed my nomadpreneur dream. The reason I was able to do it then, and why I continue to do so now, is that I have my own definition of success for myself. I have my own definition of freedom for my self. I have my own definition of happiness for my self, and I made a commitment a long time ago to live true to my self.

Choosing and acting on a different belief system is a requirement for quitting your current form of employment, turning your passion into profit and launching into the nomadpreneur lifestyle.

That's why changing your belief system is critical.

What is *your* new definition of success? How will you redefine "making it?" Will you roam the hills of Laos while your website sells digital copies of your *My Life as a Circus Performer* e-book? Will you wander the dunes of the Sahara while clients subscribe to your *How to Speak Like the French* video?

Yes, becoming a nomadpreneur requires being able to see the paradigm objectively for what it is, and being able to redefine "success in life" according to your paradigm of choice.

Required: minimalism and detachment

Reduce your expenses

Unless you remain vigilant and take specific steps against it, your expenses will always rise to meet your income. The only ways to remain above zero are to (a) make more, or (b) spend less. It's really simple.

Author T. Harv Ecker said it well in *Secrets of the Millionaire Mind*. He's the only other author I've heard advocate this. He calls it "simplification." I call it "streamlining" or "minimalism." That "spend less" option is considered almost taboo in this consumer-driven society, but it's a sensible approach to making the money you *do* have accomplish more for you. Later, I'll share with you just how minimal a nomadpreneur's monthly expenses can be.

Detach from things

The more things you own and are attached to, the less free you are.

Detach from specific outcomes

"The Universe is Perfect." That's a mantra for life that can make life go a lot smoother. Set your goals, make efforts to achieve them, but don't be so wedded to specific outcomes that you fail to recognize that more often than not, the unfolding is more perfect and divinely ordered than you could have anticipated.

Required: non-linear thinking (and action!)

Separate unconnected, non-critical tasks

When completing a project or achieving any goal in life, many people are trained to think sequentially, or in linear terms. In other words, they perform task "A" then task "B," then task "C" believing these tasks must be performed in that unique order—that the events are connected by a single line (hence the term linear). In project management, they call this finding the critical path—*"the activities that must be completed in sequential order on schedule for the entire project to be completed on schedule."* For instance, in the task of constructing a house, the two activities "build the walls" and "attach the roof" *must* be done sequentially, and a delay in the first will affect the completion of the second. These two tasks, therefore, are said to be on the critical path.

However, an important skill to develop in order to construct your new life, is the ability to think in a *non- linear* fashion and separate unconnected events. Some activities/events are, in fact, on the critical path to reaching a goal, but others are not, and being able to identify those unconnected, non-critical tasks can be liberating. Let me give a simple example of how this might apply to nomadpreneuring.

Many people believe they have to actually *write* a book before they can *sell* it. It seems like a logical progression. The truth is that these two events—the completion and the selling—are actually unconnected. You can, in fact, pre-sell a book, and start collecting money months before your book actually exists—earning nomadpreneurial income from sales to fund your travel before you've written a single word!

Many years ago, satisfied customers who bought my book about starting a record label, began to contact me requesting that I write a similar book about starting an artist management company. I listened, and before writing the book, I sent out an order form requesting that customers send their money in advance, and that I would fill their orders in two to three months when the book was complete. Guess what? They did, and I was able to finance the printing of my second book with money from customers who purchased on their faith in my promise to follow through.

Experiences like that helped me understand that certain events I thought were connected weren't really connected at all in reality, but merely in my mind, and that if I could separate them in my mind, I could accomplish much more, move forward quickly, create momentum, and achieve the results I desired.

Business is full of opportunities like this to move forward in non-traditional, counter-intuitive ways; ways that allow you to get from point A to point D while filling in points B and C later on!

Here's another example. Let's suppose you are in the process but have not yet been approved for your credit card merchant account. However, someone calls you today to place a credit card order. What would you do? Many people would tell the potential customer, "Sorry, we can't accept credit cards right now. Can you send a check instead?" Result: you might receive a check a few days later, but you absolutely lose the immediate sale (with no guarantee that the customer will take the time to follow through).

Here's how a bold, non-linear-thinking nomadpreneur would handle it. She would thank the customer, gladly take the order, the credit card information, expiration date, CVV number, billing address and shipping address. She might inform the customer that the order will ship in a few days, giving her enough time to complete the merchant vendor application, charge the card, and ship it out. Or, she might even take the chance and actually ship the order out and hope that the customer's card is valid when she eventually charges it at some point in the future. Result: she makes an immediate sale.

Non-linear thinkers realize you don't need to actually have the merchant account in place in order to take the credit card order. For that matter, you don't need to have anything at all in place to take orders.

You can separate *selling* a book from actually *having* a book to sell. You can separate *accepting* credit card orders from actually *having the means* to charge the card. And, you don't need to "have enough money" before you quit your job to become a nomadpreneur. These steps are not connected in sequence by a single line. They can be executed in a parallel (side by side).

Of course, acting on this way of thinking requires a certain tolerance for risk and uncertainty, and this sometimes causes people to worry:

What if I don't finish the book on time?
Answer: Send the pre-paid customers an apology letter and offer them some sort of bonus for their patience. Refund anyone who gets nasty.

What if my merchant account isn't approved?
Answer: Take the loss, or simply contact the customer and ask for a different form of payment.

Practicing non-linear thinking and the art of separating unconnected events requires that you be confident about your ability to fulfill your promises, honor your commitments, complete a cycle of action and get things done in a timely manner. It requires that you have a clear vision of where you're heading, the confidence to know you will get there, and, that if for some reason things don't work out the way you anticipate, it's not the end of the world.

As long as you have a "plan b" and are comfortable with any scenario that results (i.e. printing delay, refunding the order, loss of sale), you and your reputation will survive. There's no death penalty.

As you create your nomadpreneur lifestyle, ask: *"Do I really need to do A before B? Can I do C (my actual goal) first, and then come back later and do A?"* You'd be surprised just how creative and successful you can become (don't break any laws) by simply separating unconnected events and becoming a non-linear-thinking nomadpreneur!

Yes, becoming a nomadpreneur requires the ability to separate the unconnected events in your strategies.

Required: raise your belief level

Let's imagine I'm your business coach and advisor, and you've come to me with an idea for a product or service you want to sell by launching a passion- centered business around it as quickly as possible. I say,

"It does NOT take years, months, weeks, or even days to start a business and start making money. We can do it in hours, or even minutes, and I'm going to show you how!"

Would you believe me? Well, the fact is: even though this is a practical, how-to guide designed to achieve a specific outcome, the key to your success in this or any endeavor is not a matter of actions but one of belief. In other words the people who will succeed at launching a passion-centered business quickly and turn their passions into profit, and become nomadpreneurs are the people who embark on this journey with the belief and conviction that it is possible to do so.

If you do not believe a goal is possible for you, you can implement all the steps in the world, and still not be successful. Why? Success is not simply about completing a series of steps. Your belief level affects the thoughts you think. Your thoughts influence your confidence, your courage and your creativity. Your creativity determines the types of ideas you come up with, the colors you choose for your site and logo, the words you use in your headlines and sales copy, and a whole set of specifics and intangibles that will affect your success. In other words, people who "believe" they will succeed act more confidently, take more risks, create more dynamic products, and use different words to communicate than people who don't believe. It makes sense, doesn't it? Therefore, anything you can do to raise your belief level will help improve the quality of your product, your sales copy, your website, and thus the overall impact of your business. To raise your belief level, I suggest you read about other successes, seek out and speak with people who are doing what you wish to do, take self-help courses, read, listen or watch informational and inspirational books, videos and audio CDs, and generally immerse yourself in the world of entrepreneurial success.

The ideal scenario would be to find someone who's already doing what you wish to do who can coach you. Now, I'd love to be able to coach everyone, but since, practically speaking, I can't, this manual will serve as a way for me to be your virtual coach to help you raise your belief level.

Suggested: embrace technology (a bit more)

Though not absolutely required (Luddites can be nomads, too!), nomadpreneuring can be made easier the more willing you are to embrace technology. If smartphones, Skype, mobile-ready, social media, Youtube, Facebook, Twitter, apps, websites and blogs are not part of your reality or working vocabulary, then you'd be wise to start the learning curve right away.

Luddite: n. 1. historical. a member of any of the bands of English workers who destroyed machinery, especially in cotton and woolen mills, that they believed were threatening their jobs (1811–16). 2. a person opposed to increased industrialization or new technology

Congratulations! Now that you've read my story of what's possible; discovered the historical context of nomadpreneuring; started thinking about what type of location-type nomadpreneur you shall become; sent out the call to your courageous, disciplined self; made a commitment to live true to your self; stepped back far enough to recognize the insanity of the prevailing paradigm; begun to question and redefine what success means to you; broken ground on constructing the foundation of a better belief system; jettisoned the expenses, objects and attachments that could weigh you down and hold you back; developed an outline of a plan with unconnected, non-linear events; agreed to challenge and raise your current belief level about what's possible; and are willing to embrace and overcome any lingering resistance to technology and the liberation it offers--you have thereby begun the mindset evolution process--from my perspective-- required to become a nomadpreneur!

Welcome to the adventure!

Now, let's talk money!

SECTION II: MONEY ▲

Chapter 4: Method [toc]
The fundamental, underlying structure

The fundamental structure of every income strategy —the method of making money—is the same whether you are operating a brick and mortar store in Madagascar or nomadpreneuring across Antarctica. In every instance, you will need:
- a business entity
- a product (or service)
- a way to communicate its value to the world
- a way to exchange value (i.e., accept payment)

A business entity

Assuming you intend to report your income and pay taxes on it, you'll want to have this. However, fulfilling this requirement is not complicated. Most countries allow "individual" or "sole proprietor" as valid, recognized business entities and, in the US, your social security number is acceptable as your "tax id." In other words, you were born a business entity!

A product

product - *n. a high quality object or service in the hands of a consumer in exchange for a valuable. It's not really a "product" until it is exchanged.*

As described in *Turn Your Passion Into Profit*, your product may be based on your own (or another's) creativity or expertise and may take one of these forms:

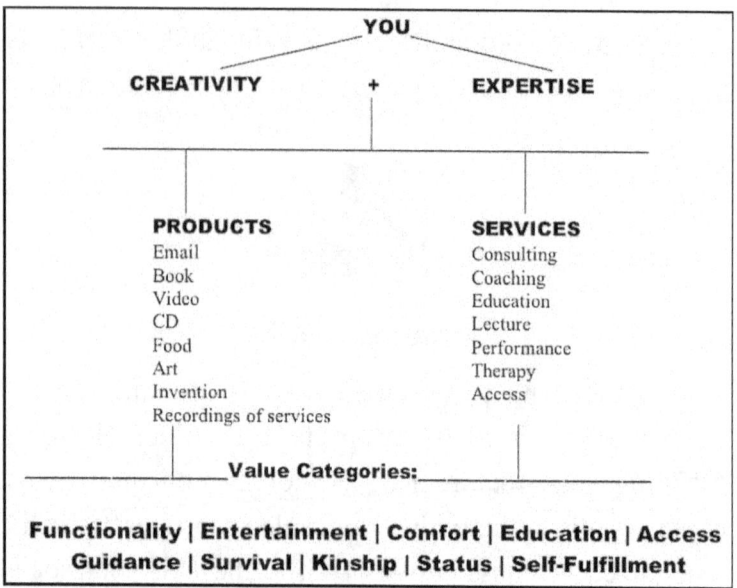

The value categories are the underlying wants and needs that your product fulfills for the consumer. This is the actual value they are paying for.

A way to communicate value

Communication is the catalyst for cash. In its most rudimentary form, you need some way to let potential customers know that your business entity as well as your product exist, that you're open for business, and to demonstrate how their lives will be better (which one or more of the value categories will be satisfied) by making a purchase.

In its basic form, this can be your presence on a street corner with a box of fruit and a "for sale" sign, or your voice shouting "Get your fresh fruit here!"

To communicate your product's value to the world in our new, technology-embracing, nomadpreneur paradigm, you'll need one or more of the following: a website or other online presence (blog, ebay listing, Craig's List post, Facebook ad), a social network account (Twitter, Facebook, Youtube, Instagram, etc.), and/or text or email capability.

A way to exchange value

Lucky for you, the world has already agreed that money is the way we exchange value. You don't have to print your own currency or develop a new method.

Once again, keeping it simple, all you really need is the palm of your hand, a bucket, a hat, a wallet or a pocket to accept payment for your product or service.

However, in our new mobile-friendly, digital paradigm, the following will be helpful:
- a bank account
- merchant status
- a "shopping cart" or other money acceptance system (COD / Western Union / Paypal Anywhere)

Paypal Anywhere turns your phone into a credit card terminal.

Simply plug it in, swipe the customer's card and get paid on the spot, on the street corner, in the hostel, etc.

QUESTION: What if I just want to keep it simple???

Ok. Here's a simple example

All strategies—whether old or new—are simply variations of the fundamental "entity / product / communication / exchange" structure. Let's apply it to a simple example. Imagine that a nomadpreneur arrives at a new destination, goes diving along the beach to gather shells, and then he sells seashells by the sea shore. Here's how our fundamental structure would translate in this location-specific scenario:

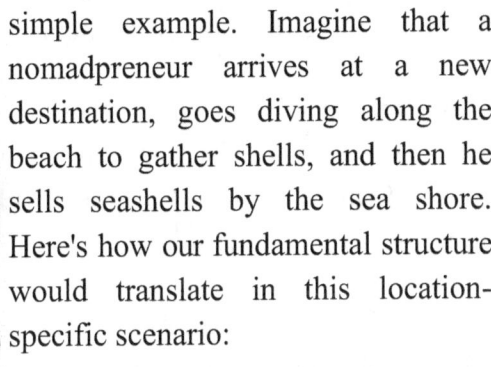

Basic business structure	Declaring earned income; Paying individual taxes
Product	Sea shells
Way to communicate value	Voice *("Get your sea shells right here!")*
Way to exchange value	Hands; pocket; wallet

Always remember the simplicity of it all.

How to use these strategies

Next, I'll share some specific nomadpreneur strategies. Their viability changes as new technologies emerge, companies change their user policies and as the buying public changes its habits. I've used most of these strategies at some point over the years, so here are some tips for getting the most from them:

Tip: For every "Start here" resource mentioned in these strategies, others exist that may be operating under the radar. Search online for "sites like Crewbay," for instance, to find similar sites.

Tip: Make it your goal to visit each of these sites. Visit pickingjobs.com even if you're not interested in picking fruit as a strategy. Reading about one strategy may spark an idea for another, and you'll often find links to other resources that may be of interest.

Tip: Unless specifically identified otherwise (.net, .org or other), site services are all .com. (eg. Gofundme = gofundme.com)

Tip: The world of travel sites, advice and resources is ever changing and evolving. This set of ideas should be considered a gateway into this world.

My request: Share *your* tips and strategies with others in the comments at passionpreneur.com/blog

Chapter 5: Strategies [toc]
*Get paid directly by customers
or by a single entity on their behalf.*

Any income you ever receive--other than inheritances and lottery winnings--will fall into one of three categories:

1. earned income - from any activity that pays based on time and effort spent; includes working a job, owning a small business, consulting and gambling.

2. portfolio income - from selling an investment for a higher price than you paid for it. This, what the IRS refers to as "capital gains," includes trading stocks, bonds, mutual funds, CDs, T-bills, currency, futures, real estate, antiques and collectibles.

3.passive income - from investments, intellectual property or businesses that don't require your time/effort; includes rental income, book/music royalties, patents, turnkey online businesses, network marketing income from your downline organization.

Passive income is usually also recurring, meaning you do the work putting it in place one time, and it keeps generating income month after month, year after year. We call that *passive residual income*. This is the ideal strategy for nomadpreneurial freedom and shall be our first focus.

Strategy 1. Create rental income

One of the best ways to free yourself to become a nomadpreneur is to create a dependable stream of passive rental income at home before you leave. Rental income from a reliable tenant paying monthly (or even for six months or a year in advance) may be just what you need to become a location-free nomadpreneur. Hopefully, you'll have enough left over after expenses (mortgage, maintenance, upkeep etc.) to finance all or part of your nomadpreneur adventure.

Your business entity can be "individual." Your product, ("a place to live,") sells itself. Communicate its availability in newspaper ads, Craig's List or through your social network. Your tenant can pay you via Paypal so you have access to the funds wherever you go.

Depending on the demand in your neighborhood, you may also consider renting out your place as a vacation accommodation independently or through a service like Airbnb.com. It's not unusual to charge and receive several times the daily regular residential rate. If the regular monthly rental price in your neighborhood is $900/month, that's $30/day. A traveler could easily spend $100/night at a budget hotel. So, if you charged the same $100/night, then in only 9 days of occupancy, you could earn what you would otherwise earn in 30 days renting to a regular tenant. Yes, the potential is there to earn more money per day, but the occupancy may not be dependable. Your apartment/home might sit empty for weeks or months without a customer. Is it better to rent to the tourist for more money but less reliability, or rent to the tenant for less and have a reliable stream? Your choice.

N-Type: location-free
Income: passive; monthly/weekly (or as agreed upon)
Tip: *Need cash up front? Offer your tenant a discount if they pay for several months in advance.*

Strategy 2. Generate other types of passive income

As mentioned, income that keeps coming without any effort on your part is called *passive income*. You do the work or create the product once, but keep earning income passively over and over again. Royalties from intellectual property (books, patents, syndicated tv/movie performances, music, etc.), affiliate or network marketing income and any business that doesn't require your direct efforts are all sources of passive income. (Income requiring ongoing effort is *earned income*.)

To earn passive income, you could also:
- Earn interest from peer to peer lending through sites like Prosper and LendingClub.
- Sell your photos on Shutterstock, iStockphoto, etc.
- Monetize your Youtube videos
- Develop and sell a unique app
- Create and charge for access to an online course through a site like Udemy

N-Type: location-free
Income: passive; immediate, monthly

Strategy 3. Stir a *passive* whirl into an *earned* stream

This tip is so powerful that I decided to make it a strategy unto itself!

Many of the income strategies that follow involve some degree of continuous effort in order to sustain them. In other words, they are mostly examples of earned income. The smartest thing you can do as you read each one is to ask yourself, *"How can I add a passive component to this?" "How can I create a book, a manual, a guide, an audio product, a video, a show, a documentary, an online course (filmed/recorded while performing the activity) that I can sell separately to the same or different clients?"*

For example, offering tours is an earned income strategy; you get paid once for doing the tour, and then

the money stops. What if, however, you film yourself and/or your clients during these tours, then monetize those videos on Youtube, or sell them to the same clients, or to elderly or disabled folks who can't make or afford the trip to Antarctica, but who will gladly pay $29.95 (plus shipping) for a virtual tour!
N-type: location-free
Income: passive; immediate

Strategy 4. Teach a language abroad

Teaching a language is typically a location-bound income strategy. In other words, the value you offer your students is more than just your ability to speak and teach a language; it's your physical presence as, say, a native English-speaking foreigner in their homeland. Your students enjoy your physical presence, your mannerisms, your energy and the opportunity to interact with you in person.

However, once you establish that initial presence in a particular location, you could easily continue to teach the language via Skype once you depart. Or, as is increasingly common in this digital age, you could establish, nurture and grow a clientele of students entirely online without ever meeting them in person!

Type: location-bound; location-free
Income: earned; immediate
Start here: goabroad.com, eslcafe.com
Tip: *Set up recurring payments for several individuals via Paypal and teach weekly classes via Skype; record the sessions via MP3SkypeRecorder and sell to others.*

Strategy 5. Teach ANYTHING abroad

Teach how to play a musical instrument. Teach yoga. Coach fitness. Teach hip hop dance (*any* type of cultural dance) to other cultures. Teach surfing at the beach, scuba diving, even how to self-publish books!
N-type: location-bound
Income: earned; immediate
Tip: *Work in public parks and where the travelers are.*

Strategy 6. Become a tour guide

Have you fallen in love with a particular destination or region and want to share your knowledge, familiarity and passion with others? Becoming a tour guide might offer the path to nomadpreneurial freedom! The great part is you can charge just about anything you believe you're worth. Really! If you have something unique to offer your potential tour clients that they can't get anyplace else—say, the only French speaking guide with a PhD. in Oceanic culture in this part of New Zealand—you've got the "French tourists to New Zealand market in your pocket!"

You can set up your own website, sign up as a guide with ToursbyLocals or Viator, or do all three.

N-Type: location-bound
Income: earned; $100+ per tour; immediate
Start here: toursbylocals.com
Tip: *Add yourself to the **wikitravel.org** page for your destination. Set up a free website through **wix.com***

Strategy 7. Sell stuff on eBay

Sell your art. Sell other people's art. Sell products from one location to customers in another. I have a Filipino friend who set up an online store, and from his location in Asia, sells culturally-familiar products to OFWs (Overseas Filipino Workers) globally.

N-Type: location-bound; location-free
Income: earned; immediate
Start here: ebay.com

Strategy 8. Become a "Kindlepreneur"

My most popular books sell more as Kindle editions than as paperbacks. For every 100 books I sell, 67 will be for Kindle or as pdf ebook, and 33 will be paperback. It's absolutely free to set up a Kindle author account, and you can even pre-sell your books before you've written a single word. You could become a New York Times bestseller without ever printing a single physical book! Think I'm kidding? Check out the profile on Darcy Chan on the next page. Darcy isn't a nomadpreneur, but that's probably because she hasn't read *my* book yet. What matters is the potential for mobility that exists as a kindlepreneur.

Note: *While I use the term "Kindle--", I'm referring to all types of digital editions (pdfs, Nook, Mobi, etc.)*

N-Type: location-free

Income: passive; immediate, monthly

Start here: Set up accounts at kdp.amazon.com smashwords.com, nookpress.com **Tip:** *write articles to promote your books; send review copies to bloggers interested in your genre.*

Profile: Darcy Chan, Kindle Kaboom!

The novel took 2½ years to write. After seeking feedback from family and friends, she sent queries to more than 100 literary agents. Most rejected it as a tough sell. "It didn't really fit any genre," Ms. Chan says. "It has elements of romance, suspense, mystery, but it falls into the catch-all category of literary fiction, and of course that's the most difficult to sell."

This past May, Chan decided to digitally publish it herself, hoping to gain a few readers and some feedback. She bought some ads on Web sites targeting e-book readers, paid for a review from Kirkus Reviews, and strategically priced her book at 99 cents to encourage readers to try it....

Sales kept climbing. In July, it sold more than 14,000 copies. That month, it was featured on two of the biggest sites for e-book readers, generating a surge of new sales. In August, it sold more than 77,000 copies and hit the New York Times and USA Today e-book best-seller lists; it later landed on the Wall Street Journal list. In September, it sold more than 159,000 copies. To date, she has sold around 413,000 copies. She's now attracting bids from foreign imprints, movie studios and audio- book publishers, without selling a single copy in print. [*Wall Street Journal article by Alexandra Alter*]

Strategy 9. Sell location-free digital products

Create cartoon graphics for authors. Compose background music for movie directors. Do translation services for lawyers. Proofread letters for business owners. Review blueprints for contractors. Write contracts for musicians. Then deliver the finished product via email, ftp (file transfer protocol), the cloud, DropBox or similar service or shared network. You are limited only by your courage.

N-Type: location-free
Income: earned; unlimited; immediate
Tip: *Set up your own website or use any of the freelancing sites that exist*
Start here: Upwork.com Fiverr.com, Guru, Task Army.

Strategy 10. Consult remotely and virtually

As a variation of the previous strategy, consider offering your passion and/or area of expertise by email, phone, skype, fax or a combination of all of these. You can give dating advice via Skype, business consulting by phone, or virtual office assistance by efax

and email all while on the road!
N-Type: location-free
Income: earned; immediate
Start here: Join the freelance sites mentioned earlier.

Strategy 11. Design and customize websites

Use your techie super powers and knowledge of HTML, Javascript, PHP, Perl and other programing languages to design or customize websites for singers, artists and even other nomadprenurs! Join the super smart community at StackOverflow for support and answers completing any coding you're unfamiliar with. You don't have to be the best, you simply have to know where to find the answers!
N-Type: location-free
Income: earned; immediate
Start here: join the freelance sites mentioned earlier.

Strategy 12. Sell location-bound physical products

There are markets around the world where you can rent a stall and sell to tourists and other travelers. Offer your own passion-centered, hand made crafts, artwork or clothes from other countries.
N-Type: location-bound
Income: earned; variable; immediate
Tip: *create a website and hand out business cards to create location-free income.*

Major Tip: If your strategy requires you to have a physical address to receive mail or packages *and* have them forwarded to you on the road, *and* if you can't or don't wish to rely on friends or family, **start here**:
- mailboxforwarding.com
- earthclassmail.com
- travelingmailbox.com
- Amazon Lockers (US locations only)

***

Nomadpreneur Profile: A king in Thailand

There's this guy who lives the untethered lifestyle in Thailand. He's a US expat who escaped to live in the land of his dreams. So, how does he support himself? Well, once a year, he takes a batch of scarves and shawls and other items from Thailand, to an annual convention/flea market in the states, sells all his stuff, and—because of the currency exchange rate—makes enough to live like a king for another year!

***

Strategy 13. Busking (street performing)

If you're thinking: *"To heck with all this digital stuff! I want to be like the circus performers!"* fear not, that lifestyle exists, and it's called busking. Busker is a mid-19th century, word for a street performer who plays for donations. (from the Spanish *buscar*, which means "to seek.") Each country has its own rules for busking.

N-Type: location-bound
Income: earned; unlimited; immediate
Tip: *Keep your income hat, instrument case or box visible and primed with a few bills and coins to encourage contributions!*
Start here: buskersadvocates.org, streetslive.org

Strategy 14. Set up your own worldwide tour

Like busking, but with more preparation and advanced marketing is touring. Perform solo or in a band in destinations that interest you! Become a guest lecturer and arrange your own international book release/speaking tour. Visa rules apply.
N-Type: location-bound
Income: earned; variable
Tip: *monetize the Youtube videos of your shows*

Strategy 15. Take your passion/talent/training on the road offering traveler-focused services

Some passion pursuits can be accomplished remotely without meeting your customers. However, if your passion requires your physical presence and interaction with your clients, then take it on the road!

What services do other travelers want or need? Massages near resorts. Face painting at summer camps. Translations, haircuts and manicures at hostels. Set up your nomadpreneur shingle at these and other places travelers congregate. Certain non-solicitation and license rules may apply, so it would be best to get permission from the municipality or business owner.

N-Type: location-bound
Income: earned; variable; immediate
Tip: *put up signs at neighboring hostels; work with local tour guides offering commissions for referrals; secure your clients BEFORE you get there.*

Strategy 16. Edit bad English signs/menus

I found this on Wandering Earl's website and loved it! As a writer and stickler for good grammar (please overlook any missed typos in this book!) I've often commented on the need for such a service.

"It might sound silly but there are travelers out there earning decent money by wandering around touristy areas all over the world and getting paid to correct the

English spelling/grammar on signs and menus of businesses that try to attract foreigners. I met one guy in Thailand who would charge $10 for his editing services and he would have approximately 20 clients per week. Not a bad way to earn $800 bucks per month."

N-Type: location-bound

Income: earned; variable; immediate

Tip: *include (or rubber stamp) "signs by you; email" on every menu or sign you correct.*

Strategy 17. Nomadize an existing business

Ever heard of a traveling electrician? Plumber? Masseuse? Beautician? Fitness Instructor? No? Doesn't matter. Create your own reality. Whether it's a passion-centered business or a business you just happen to own at the moment, take that skill set on the road! There's a demand for just about any service everywhere in the world. All you need is a way to let people know where you'll be and when. That's where a good social network, Craig's List, Couchsurfing, or any online forum can be useful.

Type: location-bound

Income: earned; immediate

Strategy 18. Monetize a travel blog

People throw this idea around all the time. However, in my opinion and experience, it takes quite a bit of commitment and discipline (and perhaps a real techie) to really maximize the income potential. However, if you *can* make it work by generating a following for your blog posts, it can be a great source of income through selling advertising, doing product endorsements and marketing your own products. You can deal directly with your advertisers, or use advertising aggregators who typically pay out monthly.

N-Type: location-free
Income: passive; variable; monthly
Tips: monetize Youtube videos, too; sell text links
Start here: Problogger.com; textlinkbrokers.com

Strategy 19. Monetize *any* kind of blog

Your blog doesn't have to be about travel just because you're a nomadpreneur! Blog about anything that interests you and create following!

N-Type: location-free
Income: passive; variable; monthly
Tips: *monetize Youtube videos, too; sell text links*
Start here: Problogger.com; textlinkbrokers.com, linkworth.com

Strategy 20. Become an affiliate marketer

Even though affiliate marketing is just one way to monetize an online presence, many people have used it as their sole strategy for generating income without any blog or content to support it. Place a specially- formatted link on your website that directs a website visitor to a particular product on a vendor's site. When someone clicks on that link, and if they ultimately purchase that product (or others), you earn a commission for the referral. Many established online companies offer affiliate programs.

A techie who knows how to optimize her website to appear prominently in search engine queries for "best luggage for nomads" could use this strategy well.

Type: location-free
Income: passive; variable; typically monthly
Start here: Amazon.com

Strategy 21: Drop ship with manufacturers

Set up a drop ship arrangement with product manufacturers. As the "middle man/woman" all you have to do is take the order from the customer, then have the manufacturer actually fulfill the order.

N-Type: location-free
Income: earned; variable; immediate

***

Profile: The Drop Ship Genius

"How does he make any money selling the computer parts at such ridiculously low prices?" I asked my friend.

"Ah, that's the genius of it," he replied. "It's not about the products at all."

I was anxious to hear the details. David always had interesting tales about people he'd met during his travels around the world. We'd been talking about income strategies and he told me about Mustafa, a techie who was drop-ship selling container-loads of computer supplies to buyers overseas. He was gaining tremendous market share because he was selling his products just above wholesale and undercutting his competitors.

"The buyers pay Mustafa in advance for the parts," David continued. "Mustafa promises to ship the parts after 60 days. He then deposits the money in an interest-bearing account. Sixty days later, after earning interest, he pays the manufacturer who then drop ships to the buyer. Mustafa never takes possession of the parts, and simply earns his money on the interest."

That's the sort of nomadpreneur strategy just about anyone could execute while sipping coconut water on a beach in the middle of the Pacific!

***

Strategy 22. Maximize "Fulfillment By Amazon"

FBA, or Fulfillment by Amazon takes "buy low, sell high" drop shipping within reach of just about anyone. The concept is a simple one: find products you'd like to sell, send them to Amazon, and they handle the storage, sales, shipping and customer support. Take advantage of Amazon's worldwide reach, low-cost shipping agreements with major delivery companies and its reputation.

N-type: location-free

Income: earned; monthly

Tip: *FBARockstars' Amazon FBA-step by step for Beginners*

youtube.com/watch?v=EIXnW-Bw0Qg

Start here: services.amazon.com/fulfillment-by-amazon/benefits.htm

Strategy 23. Internet poker

Internet poker and online games of chance could provide income for lucky (or skilled) nomadpreneurs.

N-type: location-free

Income: earned; immediate

Start here: top10pokersites.net

Strategy 24. Day trading

Buy and sell stocks to create the untethered freedom to roam.
N-Type: location-free
Income: portfolio; immediate
Tip: *invest in companies with which you're familiar and whose products you use.*

Bonus Strategy 25. Drive for Uber abroad

In theory, ride sharing--securing transportation through mobile apps like Uber and Lyft--would be a cool way to make money in different countries.

In reality, however, resistance to this new paradigm of taxi service in certain cities around the world has been severe. Drivers have faced protests by taxi drivers who complain Uber drivers should pay taxes just as taxi drivers do. Uber drivers have been fined by municipalities for violating laws requiring licenses for charging money for transporting customers. Things have even gotten violent in certain instances.

My best advice, therefore, is tread wisely and keep a watchful eye on Brazil, Canada, China, France, Germany, India, Japan, Korea and Spain where protests against Uber drivers have been most severe.

Chapter 6: Jobs [toc]

Travel continuously or change locations every few weeks while an employer pays your salary.

These strategies, while not entrepreneurial in nature, are nevertheless ways to achieve your objective of seeing the world and making money too!

Nomadize! If any job will do:

Strategy 26. Nomadize your current job

Don't care for the uncertainty of being any kind of "preneur?" Prefer an income strategy that has a bit more security and reliability with money coming from a single employer? Before you go looking for jobs with travel in the description, I would suggest first "nomadizing" your current job. Who knows? Your current employer may be open to you working remotely. Ask yourself:
• Do I really need to be in the office each day?
• Can my end product be delivered digitally?
• Can I rely on myself to produce and deliver on time without the structure of an office environment?
• Which do I value more: predictability, routine and security or randomness, variety and freedom?

Start here: set up a meeting with your boss!

Strategy 27. Get a Working Holiday Visa

Make the job search abroad a bit easier and "on the books" by simply getting a permit to work in another country for a limited time. Typically, the visa allows you to stay in a country for up to a year, and often to work in any position you wish. Australia, New Zealand, Canada, France, Ireland and Singapore offer these to foreigners, between the ages of 18 and 30.

Start here: globalgoose.com

Strategy 28. Or, just relocate already!

If you simply want a change of scenery and don't mind doing the corporate cubicle thing as long as it's in your country of choice, then simply apply for a job! Many companies have the power to pay for relocation, offer housing, sponsor work permits/visas and permanent resident status for new employees. Not exactly nomadpreneuring, but may be a direct route to the happiness you seek!

Start here: ExpatExchange.com, EscapeArtist.com

If those options aren't for you, perhaps you can apply to specific companies and organizations for which travel is a key part of the job description:

Strategy 29. Become a travel photographer

Check out this recent job opening listing at jobs.goabroad.com/search/photography/jobs-abroad-1:

"Adventure Photos is looking for experienced photographers and Chief photographers to join our talented, international team in breathtaking upscale vacation resorts around the world. The ideal candidate should have experience in wedding or session photography and preferably a degree or similar studies in the photography field. Cruise ship experience an added benefit."

Sound like something you can handle? The requirements for their Junior Photographer position are: 24 to 26 years old
• 80% English; • 6 months to 1 year experience; • Experienced in professional session/wedding
• photography equipment handling and photo editing software (Photoshop/Lightroom); • Excellent service attitude, • sales experience and prepared to work shifts
• Availability in Playa del Carmen or Cancun.
Start here: monster.com/jobs/q-travel-photography-jobs.aspx

Strategy 30. Do research for a travel guidebook

Contact the guidebook publishers directly to apply for these positions.
Start here: Google "list of travel guide books wiki"

Strategy 31. Work for the government

Here in the US, the Post Office, Federal Emergency Management Agency (FEMA), Department of the Interior, even the National Parks Service could send you to distant locations. I once met a National Park Service ranger here on Saipan who was stationed on the Midway Atoll. Assignments may take you to US possessions as well as foreign countries.

Strategy 32. Work for independent agencies and non- government organizations

Consider charities, humanitarian organizations, independent agencies like the Peace Corps, Red Cross, Doctors without Borders, Human Rights Watch, as options for seeing the world while doing good work.

Strategy 33. Become a flight attendant

The lifestyle can be a bit hectic, but opportunities exist to see the world. Contact the airlines directly as their websites will usually have a "careers" link.
Start here: flightattendantcareer.com/hiring_info.htm

Strategy 34. Work for a cruise line

Live on a luxury liner, meet people, see the world and get paid while you do it! Your first step should be to contact the cruise lines directly as their websites typically have a "careers" link. Also visit aggregator sites that monitor the industry's job situation.

Start here: cruiseshipjob.com, allcruisejobs.com

Strategy 35. Work in an international traveling show

Search event sites in various cities or ticketmaster- type sites for upcoming shows, concerts and tours,

then contact the production companies directly. You don't have to be a performer. You could be a stage hand, roadie, gopher or any part of the entourage!

Start here: Pollstar.com, the only trade publication covering the worldwide concert industry.

***

Profile: The Rainbow Connection

One of the customers for my *Coffeepot Cookbook* traveler's guide just happens to be a performer for the touring version of a very popular children's show he wants to remain nameless. He gets to make children a little happier and travels the world at the same time! My lips are sealed!

***

Still haven't found what you're looking for? Well, the fact is, any talent, skill, training, adventurism or level of desperation can be turned into money if you're willing to go to where the need is, open your mouth and ask for the position or the sale! Here are some off- the-beaten-path opportunities with a little less structure (i.e. cash...off the books)

Hey! Have you considered seasonal work?

Strategy 36. Pick fruit!

Yes, you heard me: pick fruit. This option is popular in Australia and the option exists to be paid per kilo of fruit you pick, room, board or any combination of the three.

Start here: pickingjobs.com has lists by country

Strategy 37. Find Worldwide Opportunities on Organic Farms (WWOOF)

WWOOF is a loose network of organizations in over 100 countries that facilitates placement of volunteers on organic farms. You'll need to join

WWOOF in each country you intend to visit. (Subscription fees apply; you cover travel expenses to WWOOF country, travel to/from host farms, accommodations en route, insurance, toiletries, medicines, phone/internet access, day trips. The farms provide food, lodging and opportunities to learn about organic lifestyles for a one to two-week period.
Start here: wwoofinternational.org

Strategy 38. Work at a construction site

In certain cities around the world, you might simply be able to walk up to the foreman on a construction site and offer your labor!
Start here: Googlemaps' zoomed search for construction sites near your destination of choice

Work where travelers go and toil where tourists stay as a way of traveling or staying for free:

Strategy 39. Work with local tour operators

Tour companies in certain destinations may need and pay foreigners with particular language skills or personalities to greet cruise ship visitors, meet airport arrivals and provide services to guests.
Start here: See your destination's wikitravel.org page

Strategy 40. Work at a hostel

Hostels often have a high turnover of student and volunteer employees. You may be able to earn a salary or trade your time for a free room whil1e on the road.
Start here: hostelworld.com
Tip: *Make contacts with other travelers who may provide further resources when you travel to their home countries.*

Strategy 41. Work at a resort

Travelers go to resorts. Like hostels, resorts may hire you as a receptionist at the front desk, in the hotel restaurant or other staff position (Professional chef)
Start here: Search for "resorts in [your destination]"

Strategy 42. Work at nomad-friendly bars

Bars, hostels and restaurants the world over offer cash jobs to travelers. It's a thing. They often advertise in newspapers, newsletters, and on bulletin boards at hotels and hostels.
Start here: Expatexchange for entertainment links

Strategy 43. Work at a summer camp

Kids and their parents travel too!
Start here: Search for "summer camps in [city]"

Strategy 44. Work on a yacht or sail boat

This is a way to travel for free.
Start here: CrewBay.com, DesperateSailors.com

Strategy 45. Sell timeshares

The sales departments of resorts in popular areas in Greece, Thailand, Mexico, the Caribbean or any other major resort area are always looking for good salespeople who can relate to their potential customers; Americans selling to Americans, Africans selling to Africans and so on.
Start here: Google "timeshares in [city, country]"

Money may be the preferred medium of exchange, but bartering is still a means to nomadic survival.

Strategy 46. Offer your services in exchange for....

HelpX provides an online listing of farms, homestays, ranches, lodges, B&Bs, backpacker hostels and even sailing boats that invite volunteer helpers to stay with them short-term in exchange for food and accommodation. It sidesteps visa restrictions as you aren't essentially 'paid' for 'work', but hosted in exchange for helping out.

Workaway.info provides a growing list of 1000s of active hosts in over 155 countries offering all kinds of places to stay--food and accommodations--in exchange for your unique skills for a few hours a day. Visits last anywhere from a few days to a few months.

My friend Vanxai in Laos runs a trekking and adventure business (DiscoveringLaos.com). He's gotten websites built, brochures designed and online marketing tweaked by workawayers who found him on that site. In exchange, Vanxai offers room and food and takes them white water rafting through Laos!

Start here: HelpX.com, Workaway.info

Home is where the money is!

Strategy 47. Offer house sitting services

The competition is fierce: "sitters available" outnumber "jobs available." Typically, your "pay" is simply a free place to stay. However, you can find opportunities to actually get paid if (a) the house is in an undesirable location, (b)if the sit is for a short time, or (c) if you bring or are requested to bring a unique skill set to the job--for instance, if pets are involved, or if minor maintenance or upkeep is requested.

Start here: trustedhousesitters.com

***
Profile: Nomad House Sitters

[From HeckticTravels:] Canadian couple Dalene

& Peter Heck sold everything in 2009 to travel the world, staying in other people's homes. Among other stays, they spent six months house-sitting in Honduras, and at the moment they're caring for a home in Paris, France. They say, "We've had 14 jobs in nine countries, and saved over $50,000 in the cost of accommodations as a result."

***

Strategy 48. Become an au pair

Nanny, housekeeper, babysitter, au pair, tutor, personal assistant or senior care jobs are listed together.
Start here: greataupair.com, aupairworld.com

Strategy 49. Offer pet sitting services

House sitting, pet sitting and caretaking jobs are on many care sites.
Start here: sittercity.com/pet-sitting-jobs, care.com/pet-sitting-jobs
Tip: *create a video resume so prospective clients can "meet" you before hiring for their home, children, elders or pets.*

Or, as a last resort, you can simply ask for money

Strategy 50. Crowdfund your freedom

If your cause or project is compelling enough, you just might be able to get others to pay your expenses. Crowd funding sites like GoFundme, IndieGogo and Kickstarter have helped fund millions of dollars in support to independent filmmakers, artists and others with stories to tell. Are you nomadpreneuring in order to write a book, help under-served communities, end hunger or encourage world peace? Tell the crowd funding community about it!

Similarly, you'd be surprised how effective a "donate" or "contribute" button on a blog or website can be. Each year, I offer a free event-compilation calendar through my freesummerconcerts.com website. For years it was free, then I started charging

$9.95 for the listings, but things really took off when I added a "donate" button. Last summer, one woman donated $200 in support my efforts!

Each crowdfunding site has a different formula, accepts different types of projects, offers donors different ways to pay, and pays out funds based ondifferent criteria. On Kickstarter, for instance, if you do not reach your fundraising goal, you do not receive any of the funds you may have raised during the campaign. Indiegogo lets you keep whatever your campaign raised even if the goal isn't reached. Shop around before you commit.

Start here: Kickstarter, IndieGogo and visit www.gofundme.com/travel-fundraising/ for travel and adventure campaigns and success stories

Tip: *Add a Paypal donate button and include a link on every website and outgoing email.*

Final Strategy: Mix and match

You're not limited to choosing a single strategy. Combine them in any way and in any number that suits your passions and predilections. Offer guided food tours of China during the day, do stand-up comedy and busking on the streets in the evening, all while kindlepreneuring about your passion for cats!

That's how I do it. I am a location-specific tour guide, a kindlepreneur and I offer remote, virtual consulting), plus strategies 1, 2, 3 and 9 to varying degrees help me sustain my own untethered, tech-enabled, nomadpreneur lifestyle!

When I'm in New York, I might be arranging tours for Saipan tourists who are visiting my discoversaipan.com site. When I'm in China, I might be compiling summer concert listings for people in New York who subscribe to my freesummerconcerts.com site mailing list. When I'm on Saipan I might be giving tours or consulting via Skype with clients on the US mainland or anywhere in the world. And no matter where I am, you can always find me working on a new book idea, pre-selling it while I write it, and launching it for sale on Amazon and for Kindles and Nooks.

And now, I'll share exactly how I've set it all up!

Chapter 7: Secrets [toc]

My own strategies—unplugged!

Techies roam free!

The world is set up for mobility! The more tech savvy you are, the greater will be your success at nomadpreneuring. In other words, techies get to roam (practically) free! Here are two reasons why:

Open Source Software

The number one rule of the Internet is:

For every item that someone is selling you online at a price, there exists someone else who is giving it (or an alternative) away for free!

There exists an international community of tech- savvy programmers and developers who believe that certain information, knowledge and technology should be free to the masses. These folks got together, shared and collectively developed the software "source code" (making it open to the public) with the goal of creating *"high quality programs"* as well as *"working cooperatively with other similarly minded people."*

Over the years, this movement has created brilliant programs as alternatives to popular, commercial software. Don't have money for Microsoft® Word? Get Open Office! Don't want to spend thousands for Adobe® Photoshop? Get GIMP! Free software and services can make nomadpreneuring much cheaper.

My Mac died before my publishing deadline, so the manuscript and cover for this very book were created in Open Office and GIMP on a loaner PC.

Untethered!

Up until a few short years ago, if a nomadpreneur wanted to get online, she had to find a cafe or hotel lobby with wi-fi. Nowadays, your smartphone—in addition to being a camera, calculator, FM radio, voice recorder, photo album, calendar and music player, can itself serve as a wi-fi hotspot to allow other devices (like a laptop) to get online. (Find "Tethering & Portable Hotspot" in your phone's settings menu.)

In any event, if you have the courage and discipline to try something new and become a "techie" you can roam for free (or really cheap!) *[See Appendix for list.]*

As we learned, each income strategy has four elements: (1) a business entity, (2) a product, (3) a way to communicate value and (4) a way to exchange value. Let's use that template to explain each of my own nomadpreneurial operations:

How I run my tour guide operation

MY BUSINESS ENTITY: I am a sole proprietor.

MY PRODUCT: Unique, personalized tours of Saipan and the neighboring islands of Tinian and Rota from a Jamaican, vegan, minimalist, former civil engineer, New York rat race escapee perspective.

To create my product, I use:
- my life's purpose (guru*) for sharing information
- my passion for Saipan
    - *see Turn Your Passion Into Profit*

HOW I COMMUNICATE VALUE:

I have my own site (discoversaipan.com) on which I describe the uniqueness of the tours; I also market my services through toursbylocals.com. Customers typically find me through online searches for "saipan tours", through word of mouth referrals and reviews on websites like cruisecritic.com.

To create my tour brochure cards, I use:
- Photoshop ($) or GIMP2 (free) for designing them
- Vistaprint.com ($) for printing them

To reserve and host my websites, I use:
- ionos.com (formerly 1and1.com) ($)

To communicate with/reach the general public, I use:
- Google.com SEO (search engine optimized) rank (free)
- Youtube.com channel of videos of Saipan (free)
- Inbound links from other websites (free)

To communicate with my prospective clients, I use:
- Gmail.com email account (free)
- Skype.com (skype to skype-free or to landlines-$
- QQ.com for my Chinese clients (free)

HOW I EXCHANGE VALUE:

Customers prepay for their tours through my website's OSCommerce shopping cart (open source software) with merchant services provided by Paypal. Payments are deposited to my Paypal account and easily transferred my bank account as necessary.

To accept payments from my customers, I use:
- Oscommerce.com secure shopping cart (free)
- Paypal.com business account/virtual terminal ($)

My Kindlepreneur operation

MY BUSINESS ENTITY: I am an individual.

MY PRODUCTS: I sell books, guides and manuals on a range of topics from business, health, memoir, photography and politics. They are available in kindle, nook, pdf, paperback and a few in mp3 format, and as paperbacks on Amazon through the KDP (formerly Createspace) "print on demand" platform.

To create my books, I use:
- OpenOffice(free) for manuscript
- GIMP2(free) for covers & graphics

To publish/manufacture my books, cds and dvds, I use:
- **Kindle** author account (kdp.amazon.com; free)
- **KDP (createspace.com)** author account (free)

To upload my pdfs to the Kindle Direct Platform (KDP), and shopping cart download, I use:
- **FileZilla** file transfer protocol apps (free)

Other creation programs I use are:
- **PDFshrink** to reduce pdf size prior to upload ($)

HOW I COMMUNICATE VALUE: a way to reach and communicate its value to the world - I've launched websites for each of my books and made them available on Amazon.com on which I describe them with compelling sales copy. People find me through online searches, articles on other websites, comments on forums and bulletin boards, links from other websites and word of mouth.

To reserve my domains and host my websites, I use:
- **ionos.com** ($; formerly 1and1.com)

To communicate with general public, I use:
- Facebook post boosts ($)
- Press release distribution companies (free)
- Google.com/voice number for phone inquiries (free)

To communicate with subscribers/followers, I use:
- Sendgrid.com ($)
- Facebook posts (free)
- Twitter tweets (free)

HOW I EXCHANGE VALUE: customers order through Amazon as well as through my website

To accept payments, I use:
- ionos.com to host my websites ($; formerly 1and1.com)
- OScommerce.com for my shopping cart (free)
- Paypal.com to process credit card payments ($)
- Customers may pay directly via Paypal ($)

My virtual consulting operation

MY BUSINESS ENTITY: I am an individual.

MY PRODUCT: International teleclasses and live workshops on Saipan, Guam, in China, Singapore and anywhere there's demand. My product is my experience and expertise in becoming a passionpreneur, online selling, book publishing, veganism, fasting, that I share with clients.

To host/record my call-in teleclasses, I use
- FreeConferencecall.com (free)

To conduct/record individual consulting sessions
- **Skype.com** (skype to skype-free or to landlines-$)
- **Google.com/voice** (rings to cell phone; free)

To record my live workshops, I use
- the sound recorder function of my phone (free)

To edit videos of my workshops, I use:
- **OpenShot** (free)

HOW I COMMUNICATE VALUE: I mention my availability for coaching in my books and on the website for each book. People find me through online searches, articles on other websites, links from other websites and word of mouth.

HOW I EXCHANGE VALUE: Customers pay for their sessions and teleclasses online. Attendees to in- person workshops have the option of paying cash.

To accept payments, I use:
- **ionos.com** to host my websites ($; formerly 1and1.com)
- **OScommerce.com** for my shopping cart (free)
- **Paypal.com** to process credit card payments ($)
- Customers may also send money directly via Paypal

That's how my own nomadpreneur empire functions. Sound like a big operation? Want to know how much it costs to run?

My nomadpreneur operating expenses

I've included my "home base" expenses because I'll be paying most of these even when I'm actually traveling.

Personal & Home Base

Monthly rent: $aipan level
Utilities: $75/month
Food: $300/month
Miscellaneous: $100/month

HOME BASE TOTAL: $475 + rent

Business

Paypal Virtual Terminal: $30/month1
Domain registrations: $62/month2
Website hosting: $21/month
SSL certificate $ 4/month3
Sendgrid emails $ 4/month
Wi-fi: $30/month4

TOTAL: $151/month

(1) Paypal also charges a 3.5% transaction fee
(2) 50 domains x 14.95/year / 12 = $62/month
(3) billed annually at $49/year
(4) approx $30/month through my $1/day mobile data plan.
No, I didn't forget anything! If you're wondering:
Bank Fees $0
Car note/insurance $0
PO Box rental: $0
Shopping cart $0

An hour in the life of a nomadpreneur

Whether I'm in a guest house in Laos, a villa in China, a hi-rise in New York, or an apartment on Saipan, I usually wake up early (about 4:00am) and:

I check emails, which include

• notifications from customized perl scripts that let me know who has visited my site, what country they're from, and how many total visits a particular page has received. This is particularly useful if I'm tracking downloads of a new ebook.
• customer feedback/challenges downloading ebook
• voicemail notifications from Google Voice.
• faxes/email orders from wholesalers or bookstores
• Textlinkbrokers or linkworth notices for ad buys
• requests for my tours
• order & payment notifications (the good stuff!)

I fulfill orders:

If orders were placed for the digital/ebook editions (pdf, mp3) of my products, the customers would already have downloaded them through the shopping cart. Nothing to do here except count the money!

However, if any orders were placed for paperback, cd or dvd versions of my products. I can log in to my KDP/Createspace account, and order the products to be drop shipped directly to the customer.

I check site visits:

The Extremetracking.com statistics on all my sites and blogs track any unusual activity, show where visitors are coming from and what search terms they're using to find my sites.

I monitor sales on:
- my Paypal account to make sure sales are deposited
- my Kindle account
- my Nook account
- my KDP/Amazon account
- my Smashwords and other accounts

Beyond the hour

I mentioned in Chapter 4 that communication is the catalyst for cash. If you have value to offer the world and you're not generating enough money, it means you're not communicating correctly. Beyond the hour of monitoring my operations, I also must spend time

(a) communicating or making sure that communication is happening if I'm to survive as a nomadpreneur.

(b) Communicating with tour, hotel and activity customers and sending links to make payment.

(c) Communicating with subscribers who are in my autoresponder queue. (An autoresponder is an automated, daily or weekly series of emails sent out by my site. They include a link to a product or service.)

(d) Blogging or guest-blogging on other blogs
(e) Posting to Facebook, Youtube or Twitter
(f) Publishing articles
(g) announcing teleclasses
(h) announcing in-person workshops/seminars.

All of this communication, as well as the ongoing, passive, hands-free communication that's taking place via my sites' google search engine rank, my Youtube videos, old blog posts, links on other sites and mentions in other authors' books, does four things:

- generates tour clients
- generates kindle book/cd/dvd customers
- generates coaching and workshop clients
- generates ongoing opportunities to communicate more (speaking engagements, articles, blogging)

What to do if you run out of money

QUESTION: What happens if I run out of money?

No matter how well you plan, how much you earn, how carefully you budget or how cautiously you spend, it is always possible--particularly if you're engaged in a location-bound income strategy--that your income simply won't keep up with your expenses. Then what??? I have several answers to the practical question of "what should I do if I run out of money."

Answer 1. Don't run out of money.

Answer 2. Remember the universe is perfect.

If you *do* run out of money, confront it, run towards it, embrace it, and remember: *we live in a friendly, supportive universe.* It may not appear so at first, but any obstacle you encounter while pursuing a goal is forcing you to evolve into the person you need to become in order to achieve it. You may need to:

Answer 3. Become more courageous and disciplined.

Are you allowing some fear to limit your income or increase your expenses. Are you afraid to post your "for sale" sign? ask people for the sale? approach the hostel for permission to cut hair? Step outside your comfort zone. Recognize the fears that are holding you back and I.C.E. them (Identify, Confront, Eliminate).

Answer 4. Release your ego

A wise millionaire once told me that when your ego is up here (he pointed to the ceiling), your income is almost always down there (he pointed to the floor). Are you allowing your ego to prevent you from sleeping in a hostel, busking on a street corner, asking mom for help? Get over it!

Answer 5. Work smarter.

Embrace technology. Use Facebook or Twitter. Find more efficient ways to reach more people.

Answer 6. Communicate.

You're not communicating value. You're not telling enough people what you do, how to reach you, how much you charge and how to send you money in exchange for the value you offer.

Answer 7. Fast!

Take the time to fast. Stop eating. It'll do your body good! Despite what you've been led to believe watching "Survivor" and "Naked & Afraid," the human body can survive weeks without food. (Water, however, is essential). See *Fast & Grow Young*.

Oh, wait, one more! I almost forgot:

Answer 7. Go home! (Or just get out of <u>here</u>!)

At the same time, don't be stubborn if the universe is sending you signals that a particular location-bound strategy isn't conducive to your nomadpreneurial success. It could be that the people, the timing, the location and you simply aren't the best combination, then the wisest thing to do might be to jet and set up shop somewhere else!

Remember, when challenges present themselves, it's rarely an indication that your goal is unreachable. It is almost always an indication that your goal is unreachable IF you do not evolve. The fault, dear nomadpreneur, lies not in our stars, but in our selves.

SECTION III: MOBILITY

Bonus Chapter 8: Motivation [toc]

Motivation

Why do I go abroad?
Inspired by GoAbroad.com's "Why Do I go Abroad?" Contest about my 6-month Asia adventure.

...I had an absolutely, positively, wonderful and life- changing time being "Jamaican" in China, Singapore and Laos, and blogging about it.

In addition, I hope you got something more from it than just an entertaining read. I hope it expanded your awareness and consciousness in some small way. Wherever in this world you may call "home," (even if you live in China), I hope it gave you a peek into a reality you might not have otherwise been aware of. I hope it showed you people, places and possibilities in ways that affect how you see yourself, the world, and your place, role and identity within it. I hope you can now see a little bit higher above and a little bit further beyond the misconceptions and fears that often flavor our perception of "others" and those we consider "not like us." The fact is, we have been manipulated to live in such fear.

It seems an unavoidable outcome of this manipulation, and the fractionalized, brainwashed society we live in as a result, that people are taught to, and thus become inclined to identify and separate themselves according to arbitrary and meaningless national, ethnic, racial and religious lines. We are taught to fear these supposed differences and thus we perceive "others" who are "not like us" as threats to our individual and/or collective identity, control, autonomy and survival. This fear leads to a false sense of elitism, then to bias, prejudice, preferential treatment, discrimination, and attacks of psychological, verbal and sometimes even physical nature. Yet, this is all a construct. It is not natural. We are not wired to fear, attack and ostracize others because of differences. This is all learned behavior. If you don't believe me, then simply watch young children—-before they've been brainwashed—-playing with each other. You'll observe the instinctive, communal, inclusive, welcoming "wiring" we are born with. Yes, something has been taken from us.

As on-going election/human rights protests worldwide reveal, people are ready for a change of the existing paradigm of manipulation, fear and the strategy of divide, conquer and exploit. People are agitating for change. They want to take that thing back — that thing that has been taken from our natural wiring. It can be done. It is being done! The Internet and our technological age makes possible the reality of life without borders and other arbitrary lines that separate humanity. It can be used to encourage the sort of boundary-breaking, limitless, expansive and inclusive thought and action that will unite and free us. My Jamaican in China adventure is just one of many real-life adventures that offer alternative ways to be, think and act in the pursuit of such freedom.

Now, it may be presumptuous or naive of me to hope that my little nomad adventure, a blog and a book about it can somehow contribute to the massive paradigm shift in consciousness for which the world yearns, and for which it now seems poised. However, I'll share with you a thought that caught my eye some time ago. It's a truth with which I resonate profoundly, and it represents an ideal to which my life (and this six month chronicle of my life) is testament:

"To create a just, sustainable world, nothing is more important than being able to think and act across borders. Whether our passion is protecting the biosphere or preventing war, we will succeed only if we have the passion and courage to cross the national, ideological, ethnic, and religious borders of our time." —Mark Gerzon, author, *Leaders Without Borders*

These borders Mark refers to are all arbitrary lines. They do not exist in reality. They are learned and superimposed upon the now fragmented minds and thinking of individuals who should instead be thinking and acting as a global community on a single planet.

In my naiveté, I believe that Jamaican in China has the power to plant the seed of a thought about "others" who are "not like us" that says *"Perhaps things are not as I've been led to believe. Perhaps these people are not my enemies. How do I know? Well, there's this Jamaican guy who went all the way to China, and let me tell you what he experienced. !"*

And with the single click of button or a tweet of technology, you can use this book to change someone else's perspective as well. It only takes one.

There's more of a global ideological shift going on than we may realize. The "social networking" paradigm that has existed for millennia has now been dramatically enhanced by the Internet. It has changed everything. Videos go viral, protests proliferate, movements gain momentum, and individuals are impacted in meaningful ways by a "tweet" or a "like" or a "friend," or by a single post in a forum by a single individual on a single gadget, Nook, Kindle or keyboard. Yes, my friend, keystrokes and a click can change the world!

It is from this place of sincere respect for the power of communication in general, enhanced by the potential of the internet in particular, that I travel abroad, write, blog and "share what I know so that others may grow." I hope you will fulfill my humble request to use my adventure to communicate some new possibilities to at least one other person somewhere else across the arbitrary, imaginary (and slowly dissolving) lines that seek to divide us.

If you are reading this on a Nook, Kindle, iPad or any e-reader, you have the ability in most cases to share this book electronically with others. I encourage you to do so. Feel free! Please share a link or a like or a tweet with someone in your world, and thanks for being part of my adventure! [end excerpt]

***

That's just one of my motivations for being a nomadpreneur. There are, of course, others reason. I want to have experiences. I want to be in relationships and date a variety of women. I want to experience what it's like to live in other countries.

Yes, the underlying question that permeates all my travels is "could I live here?" Given the natural things that are important to me (warm weather, sunshine, clean air, access to organic fruits and vegetables), the societal things (friendly people), as well as the household amenities (a kitchen, internet access), I make an assessment and arrive at a "yep" or "nope."

If it passes my "Yep Test" and a majority of my wants and wishes are met, I unpack and stay a while.

That's one of the reasons I stay in a place for a few months. It takes time for the bloom of the visitor paradigm to wear off and for the real rhyme, reason and rhythm of the region to take hold. And, as I've said before (and which some are tired of hearing), I'm not a tourist. A hotel is an unnatural setting. If I can get a real apartment, that makes it even better. That way, I can observe the comings and goings of regular folk. Watch how business is done, how quickly products and services are delivered, learn what the real price of things are, gender roles and dating rituals, something beyond the quick and superficial view of things you get through temporary eyes and with your boarding pass still in hand.

That's what motivates me to be nomadpreneur. The thrill of discovery. The newness of relationships. The multiplicity of identities, then sharing it all with others. Yes, my motivation has been my mission!

What's *your* reason for being a nomadpreneur?

With that said and asked, let's move beyond the "why" of travel and into the when, where, how and how much of it all! Let's talk logistics!

Chapter 9: Logistics [toc]

Tips for how, where and when to travel, safety, immigration and more!

What to carry

What to carry on in order to carry on your business

Smartphone - I was a slow adapter, but have now seen the light--at least somewhat. With so many features (voice/video recorder; camera; wi-fi hotspot, FM radio, timer,) and access to apps for translation, accommodations, transportation and more, the smartphone may have redefined nomadpreneuring.

Laptop - Still, I prefer to do my writing/designing on a laptop keyboard and wider screen. However, many nomadpreneurs will be able to manage their operations with just a smartphone.

Camera (optional) I prefer the feel and quality of my small S95 Cannon. Many folks use their smartphones.

Flash drive or external drive -The video files you may be creating as you blog around the world take up a lot of space.

Health tips

My own natural traveler's first aid kit includes: *Food grade hydrogen peroxide* - disinfectant; Food grade H2O2 may be used topically and internally.

Grapefruit Seed extract - wide spectrum; kills all types of pathogens, bacteria and even viruses.

Activated charcoal capsules- good for food poisoning *Water Purification drops* - Chlorine Dioxide solution *Tea tree oil* - antiseptic for bites and stings

Zinc - for many types of bacteria and infections

Check out the book, *A Clean Cell Never Dies*, for more natural health maintenance strategies. See fastandgrowyoung.com

Money-saving travel tips

- Travel free on an airline employee's "buddy pass"
- Buy airline tickets on budget carriers; use debit or credit card offering frequent-flier miles and rebates
- Exchange your money in town, not at the airport
- Arrange with Uber drivers or Couchsurfing friends to pick you up from airport, dock, bus/train station, rest stop or side of the road
- Board for free with a couch surfing host
- Stay at hostels; offer to pay for a week/month(s) in advance to get a discount
- Shop where the locals shop
- Choose your next destination; Rinse and repeat

Dollar-a-day nomad survival tip

(Excerpt from the Jamaican in China Blog)

As mentioned, I moved to a new location—a friend's apartment in China—just before I left for Laos. However, once she returned to China, she helped me find my own, cheaper place in Xishuangbanna.

Now, as I travel and live like this in various cities in China, I'm able to establish a routine, norms and requirements for my happiness and comfort. Depending upon how "furnished" my accommodations are, I may need to purchase a few items at each destination. At my first villa in Xishuangbanna I didn't have to purchase much in the way of household items. However, this new place that my friend helped me to find was simply an empty, unused hotel room which the hotel owner equipped with a single-burner stove, and a small gas-tank to allow me to cook. Therefore, I had to buy everything else except toilet tissue.

Here's what I ended up buying, and which now constitutes my standard shopping list for new nomad destinations.

This is for those of you who think it's expensive to do what I do.

Item	RMB	USD
Sponges	1.20	0.17
Bleach	13.00	1.91
Mop	29.00	4.26
Plastic wash basin	22.00	3.23
Hooks	8.97	1.32
Manual water pump	15.00	2.22
Dustpan/broom	9.00	1.32
Dishwashing liquid	9.00	1.32
Hangers(12)	5.90	0.87
Stove adjustor	2.90	0.42
Small pot (rice)	9.95	1.46
Bulbs (3@.97each)	2.91	0.42
Cutting board	9.95	1.46
3 floor mats	15.00	2.20

Total cost in US $23.31

That's it! See? It's not that expensive at all—particularly if you're on a US-derived income. Of course it helps if you're low-maintenance minimalist, willing to shop where the local people shop, but the fact is, your dollar can go much further in many destinations.

As for cooking, I've developed a unique strategy for maintaining my vegan lifestyle as a nomadpreneur: I call it *The Coffeepot Cookbook: A Fun, Functional & Feasible Traveler's Guide to Preparing Healthy, Happy Meals on the Go Using Nothing but a Hotel Coffeepot and a Little Ingenuity!* [See Books])

So, my point is, when you think to yourself that traveling around the world is something you could never do, remember the Jamaican in China—the dollar-a-day nomad!

Safety tips

QUESTION: Is it safe being a nomadpreneur abroad?
ANSWER: It's probably safer than you fear it is. *"Foreigner Completes Safe, Fun, Relatively Uneventful, Crime-Free Adventure in Egypt."* isn't a headline you'll read in the tabloids. Most of what we read, and thus most of what we fear about other countries are the bleeding headlines—reports of kidnappings, war, strife and turmoil.

I've walked the dimly-lit streets of Hainan, China at 2 in the morning. I've trekked through the mountains of Laos on my own. I've explored the back roads of Manila on the weekends and emerged unscathed.

I believe, you will attract that which you fear. However, here are some steps you can take to increase your feeling of security:

• Check in with the local authorities and/or embassy.
• Travel with a partner
• Let someone at the hostel/hotel know your plans
• If you're a woman, don't take safety advice from a man (that includes me) as the final word.

On that last point, I'm going to suggest you get safety and travel tips from someone who looks like you. Generally speaking, an individual's experience in any country will vary depending on many factors including physical appearance and nationality.

Yes, of course you're unique. Yes, you'll

distinguish yourself from the others by your charm and unique aura. However, thanks to Youtube as well as the behavior of your own countrymen, people will often meet your nation's / culture's/ ethnicity's stereotype before they meet you. Will you be perceived as the ugly American, the free-spending Dutch? the English cheapskate? the rowdy behaving-badly Chinese, the sexy, athletic Jamaican (did I say that out loud?) and treated accordingly? Of course, as a nomad, you have an opportunity to change (for better or worse) the world's perception of whom you willingly or unwillingly represent. This may seem counter- intuitive, but as an obvious foreigner with a Jamaican passport, I'm treated overwhelmingly more positively in China than a Chinese person would be treated.

Insurance tip

QUESTION: Is there travel insurance for nomads?
ANSWER: Check out worldnomads.com and imglobal.com/en/index.aspx

Resident status tip

QUESTION: If I'm a permanent resident of [country], can I be a nomadpreneur and retain my status?

ANSWER: This answer varies by country, but in the US, the answer is yes. The United States Citizenship & Immigration Services (USCIS) website states:

If you plan on being absent from the United States for longer than a year, it is advisable to first apply for a reentry permit on Form I-131. Obtaining a reentry permit prior to leaving the United States allows a permanent or conditional permanent resident to apply for admission into the United States during the permit's validity without the need to obtain a returning resident visa from a U.S. Embassy or Consulate abroad. Please note that it does not guarantee entry into the United States upon your return as you must first be determined to be admissible; however, it will assist you in establishing your intention to permanently reside in the United States. Residents ("green card" holders) may stay out of the US and territories for up to six months without jeopardizing your status.

See: uscis.gov/green-card/after-green-card-granted/international- travel-permanent-resident

One last nomadpreneur (in training) profile

Just as I was putting the finishing touches on this book, I received a quite lengthy email from a twenty- six year old New Yorker named Ken who began with "*I have been one of your biggest fans for over three years. I have been reading your blogs and some of your books and I have decided that I am tired of sitting around and not doing anything about my situation in leaving America and getting out...*"

and ended twenty paragraphs later with:

QUESTION: The one question I have for you is, How do I start? Where do I begin? How can I become like you...in where I can make income while traveling abroad. I am intermediate level Web developer in where I can program HTML/CS/ and a little JavaScript. How can I use my skills and passions to help get myself to leave this place for good and begin the emigration process? Does teaching English give a good option? Do I need to be a proficient front-end web developer? Where do I start, can you help lead me to where I can start?--Ken.

Ken is precisely who I am writing this book for and even though many of his "one" question are answered in this book, I'll share my actual response to him as it may prove helpful as a "getting started" email consultation for others:

Hey Ken,

1. To answer your most immediate question, join Upwork, Fiverr. Taskarmy, and start accepting jobs whether you feel you're ready or not.

2. If there's a particular community of folks you're already a part of language/dating/travel who might be potential clients for your services, then add something to the signature line of your outgoing emails and anywhere you post comments: *"Need a website designed? Contact me at . Best rates on the web!"*

3. Join the community at stackoverflow.com for

support and answers completing any coding jobs you're not completely familiar with. (Perl, PHP, etc.) Remember: You don't have to be the best, you simply have to know where to find the answers.

4. Escape and freedom may require multiple strategies, find opportunities to teach English at eslcafe.com

5. The advice that I felt most moved to share with you as I was reading your email is: You do not owe anyone an explanation for your likes and dislikes, dating preferences or anything else. Embrace who you are and what you like, and do not divert ANY more energy to speaking about it. Don't explain. Don't rationalize. Don't justify. Do not let anger, frustration or the pursuit of revenge eat at you. Let it go. Focus on giving yourself what you know will make you happy as a show of how much you love yourself. Let your anticipation of the future, (not your unhappiness with the present) motivate you. Wear a smile of serenity during your escape, not a frown of frustration.

6. It's time for action. Let people stand in awe of your escape. Let people observe you and say "You remember Ken? Well, he quit whining and actually ran off to Japan! There's a guy who is comfortable with himself and his preferences."

Great hearing from you, Ken! I'm so glad that the books and my story were helpful to you!--Walt

p.s. Here are some additional checklist items:

☐ Set a date for your escape

☐ Sep a Paypal account

☐ Compose your own "Freedom Song" email

☐ Choose a country, continent, region to explore

☐ Determine if you need a visa (visahq.com) and secure as necessary

☐ If you're not a citizen, research the rules for staying out of your country of residence for extended periods.

☐ Join Couchsurfing.org and make some friends in your destination(s) of choice

☐ Sign up to various newsletters of sites on the resource list and set up accounts as appropriate for your choice of strategies (Kindle, toursbylocals, etc.)

☐ If this move marks a semi-permanent relocation, take an initial trip to your chosen destination as a "recon mission*" to check things out on the ground.

reconnaissance mission - *n.* preliminary surveying or research.

Chapter 9: Resources [toc]

120+ nomadpreneur resources mentioned in this book

Product

☐ **passionProfit.com**
Find your purpose, discover your passion, create a product, market it for profit.

☐ **kdp.amazon.com**
Amazon's print-on-demand manufacturer. Your books, cds and dvds are immediately available on Amazon.

☐ **vistaPrint.com**
Print cards, brochures, and other merchandise

☐ **udemy.com**
Launch an online course here

Communication

☐ **Skype**
Gold standard in Voice and video over IP

☐ **WhatsApp.com**
The latest chat app of choice!

☐ **Hootsuite**
Manage all your social media communication from one dashboard; schedule posts for future dates

☐ **Sendgrid.com**
Mail delivery service that gets through spam blockers

☐ **Freeconferencecall.com**
Offer group classes with this free service

☐ **Instagram**
One of the latest social media platforms

☐ **Facebook**
Most everyone is here now. Reach them here

☐ **Twitter**
If it's good enough for presidents....

☐ **CraigsList.org**
Search for everything from housing to airline tickets

Website

☐ **ionos.com**
Thousands of domain registration/hosting companies exist. I've used 1and1 for 10+ years. Use my referral link to sign up: https://www.ionos.com/?ar=1&kwk=6793973

☐ **wordpress.org**
Launch site using predesigned templates. Add third party "plug-ins" (shopping carts, email distrib.)

☐ **wix.com**
Website design platform

☐ **extremetracking.com**
A free tracker to help monitor visitors to your website

Ecommerce

☐ OScomerce.com
Open source shopping cart for selling several products. Note: X-cart.com offers a good paid option.

☐ Paypal
Keep it simple. Use Paypal's button or basic "send money" function if you have a small number of products or no need for a checkout process.

☐ Amazon
Not just a bookstore anymore! Sell services, apps and products through FBA program. Become an affiliate. http://services.amazon.com/fulfillment-by-amazon/benefits.htm See "Paypal Alternatives" later

☐ ebay
Buy and sell for income

Passive Income

☐ airBnB.com
Generate short term rental income

☐ prosper.com
Lend money to others, earn interest

☐ lendingClub.com
Another peer lending platform

Teaching

☐ goAbroad.com

☐ ESLcafe.com
Dave's ESL Cafe offers a wealth of opportunities

Tour Guide

☐ **ToursBylocals**
Earn money as a tourguide

☐ **Viator.com**
Another popular tour guide platform

Kindlepreneuring

☐ **kdp.amazon.com**
Set up your free Kindle Direct Publishing account

☐ **smashwords**
Another great direct publishing platform

☐ **nookPress.com**
Barnes & Noble's platform for Nook e-readers

Freelancing

☐ **upwork** (elance and odesk are now upwork)

☐ **fiverr**

☐ **guru**

☐ **taskArmy**

RideSharing

☐ **uber**

☐ **lyft**
Another ride-sharing option

Busking

☐ **Association of Street Performers**
streetslive.org

☐ **buskersAdvocates.org**
Support, links, resources, best locations and more

Monetize

☐ **textlinkbrokers**

☐ linkworth.com

☐ **youtube.com**
Allow ads to appear on your videos

☐ **Google Adsense**

Crowdfunding

☐ gofundme.com
☐ kickstarter.com
☐ indiegogo.com

Open source alternatives to popular software

☐ **OpenSource**
☐ **OSalt.com**

Techie

☐ **proBlogger.net**
Expert advice on making money through your blog

☐ **webmasterWorld.com**
International community of webmasters share info on how to optimize your site for search as well as income

☐ **stackOverflow.com**
Want to customize your shopping cart to send a special text based on product ordered? Need a Perl script to process your site's subscription forms? Ask questions or search answers within a community of super smart techies.

Jobs

☐ **goAbroad.com**
Features educational as well as job opportunities

☐ **aroundtheworldin80jobs.com**

☐ **pickingjobs.com**
Links employers with seasonal workers worldwide. "Travel, work outdoors, earn money, make friends"

☐ **crewBay.com**
Crewing service connecting amateur and professional yacht crew with sailing/power boats worldwide.

☐ **desperateSailors.com**
Crewing service

☐ **cruiseshipJob.com**
Find out which cruise lines are hiring

☐ **allCruisejobs.com**
Find out which cruise lines are hiring, again.

☐ **helpx**

☐ **workaway.info**
Donate time/ talent in exchange for room and board

☐ **wwoofinternational.org**
Worldwide Opportunities On Organic Farms

☐ **monster.com**
Job listings

☐ **indeed.com**
More job listings

☐ **workingtraveller.com**
Connects travelers with skills--or those with a passion to learn that skill– with hosts who need those skills.

The world of house sitting

☐ **Housecarers** (Browse free – $50/yr member)

☐ **House Sitters America** ($30/yr)

☐ **Mind My House** ($30/yr)

☐ **Luxury House Sitting** ($10/yr)

☐ **Nomador** ($85/yr or limited free membership)

☐ **Search** Facebook, Craigslist for house sitting groups

Immigration

☐ **visaHQ.com**
Find out if you need a visa for your destination

☐ **globalgoose.com**

☐ **uscis.gov** *US Citizenship & Immigration Service*

Destinations

☐ **wikitravel.org**
Research destinations before you go.

☐ **lonelyplanet.com**
A popular travel guidebook and site

☐ **tripadvisor.com**
Travelers rate hotels, destinations and more

Expat Resources

☐ **escapeArtist.com**
The original Escape From America magazine!

☐ **expatExchange.com**
Empowers expats to help each other via articles, country forums, property/job/resource listings, more

Transportation

☐ **wikitravel.org/en/round_the_world_flights**
Round the world tickets

☐ **wikitravel.org/en/Discount_airlines**
Discount Airlines

☐ **bootsnAll**
Plan and purchase complex travel, such as around the world trips, and multi-stop international trips

Accommodations

☐ **couchSurfing.org**
A global network of people willing to host travelers!

☐ **hospitalityClub.org**
Another global network of hosts

☐ **hostelworld.com**
Find all the hostels around the world

☐ **Airbnb.com**
Find accommodations in many countries

☐ **Agoda.com**
Accommodation bookings.

Language

☐ **Google Translate (translate.google.com)**
My friends in China think I've mastered communicating in Mandarin characters! If they only knew!

☐ **Duolingo.com**
Learn primarily European languages: Spanish, French, German, Italian, English, Portuguese, Dutch, Irish, Danish, Swedish, Russian, Polish, Romanian, Greek, Esperanto, Turkish, Vietnamese, Hebrew, Norwegian, Ukrainian, Hungarian, Welsh.

☐ **Foreign Service Institute (FSI) courses**
The FSI language courses are arguably the best free language courses available anywhere--over 40 languages. See: livelingua.com/fsi-language-courses.php

☐ **Chinesepod**
Here's where I got my start learning Chinese!

Shopping

☐ **Nextag.com**
Compare prices before you purchase anything online
☐ **smalldog.com**
They ship macs worldwide!

Publications

☐ **International Living Magazine**
All the resources you need for living abroad

Emergency Insurance

☐ **worldNomads**
Offers insurance
☐ **imGlobal**
Air ambulance service

Vagabonds

☐ **WanderingEarl.com**
Derek's long term travel lifestyle blog
☐ **ExpertVagabond.com**
Matthew Karsten's expert traveler blog
☐ **JamaicaninChina.com**
Don't call me a vagabond! Vagabondpreneur, if you must!

Communities

HappierAbroad.com
Winston Wu's global dating and living community

Paypal alternatives

☐ **Google Wallet**
Formerly Google Checkout; rapid transfers to/from your bank account; credit card processing and invoices.

☐ **WePay**
Reportedly good customer service and fraud protection; offers virtual terminal; customers make purchases without leaving your site.

☐ **2CheckOut**
Merchant account with payment gateway; receive credit card and PayPal; international payments, shopping cart, and recurring billing.

☐ **Skrill**
Formerly Moneybookers; free setup, low fees; send text messages from your account. International merchants can transfer balance to prepaid debit card.

☐ **Intuit**
Accept payments online and in-person pay employees, calculate payroll taxes, and file payroll tax forms.

☐ **ProPay**
Receive, send money worldwide; recurring billing; built-in shopping cart; accepted by eBay. Offers a mobile phone credit card reader to process credit/debit cards in real-time for in-person transactions.

☐ Click2Sell
Accept PayPal, Google Checkout, Skrill, and credit cards with or without a merchant account; affiliate tracking, reports, and automated sales management.

☐ Dwolla
Pay friends, send, receive and request business payments (free); bank transfers, Automated Clearing House (ACH) payments (flat fee per mo)

☐ Braintree
Payment gateway, recurring billing, credit card storage, merchant account for online/mobile business

☐ ClickBank
A one-stop shop for online businesses since 1998

☐ Stripe
Removes the need for a merchant account or gateway.

Miscellaneous

☐ NationalStereotypes.com
Here's how people see you! A comprehensive list of how citizens of just about every country (even yours!) are perceived and portrayed in other countries. There is always some truth in stereotypes.

☐ thePennyhoarder.com
Great resource for ways to save money and make money, including ways to incorporate travel into it!

Nomadpreneur: of love and logistics
A closing thought

If you've determined that becoming a nomadpreneur is an experiment and experience you'd like to pursue, how shall you make it happen? If you've decided that the adventure of this lifestyle is the next phase in your evolution, how shall you take the next step?

Philosophers will tell you there are only two causal emotions in the universe—only two reasons we do (or don't do) anything: *love* and *fear.* Others will suggest that *most* of what we do as individuals and as a society is based on some sort of fear—fear of starvation, fear of the elements.

When it comes to becoming a nomadpreneur, those who "dream it" but never actually "do it", are often paralyzed by fear of the unknown: *Is it safe? Will I make enough money? Will I be accepted? Is there racism abroad? How will I negotiate the culture and the language?*

Then, there are those who come to this book because they're ready, or "on the fence" and in need of a little push. For them, it may be a matter of logistics: *What apps are available? What should I carry? What's the best strategy? Where is the opportunity? Where should I stay? How do I get cheap tickets?*

For those love-challenged and fear-focused individuals, I've done my best, in this book as well as my travel blog, to address issues of safety, survival and acceptance by offering my own experiences and the examples of others who are living the nomadpreneur experience.

For individuals at a loss for logistics, I've done my best to itemize the necessary strategies, steps, and resources required for execution.

From my own experience, I believe a healthy mix of love as well as logistics is often at play and ultimately required to move a person to action: *Do I love myself enough to take action to do this thing that will make me happy? Do I fear the alternative and regret of not taking action enough? What's the best plan of action?*

I hope *How to Become a Nomadpreneur* will answer those questions, and serve as inspiration to begin the journey in pursuit your dreams!

You are now free to roam about the planet!

Your friend in freedom, Walt F.J. Goodridge

p.s. MY steps for how to become a nomadpreneur

1. Find courage/discipline to live a better belief system
2. practice veganism (stop eating garbage and poison)
3. maintain youth, perfect health & long life
4. reclaim your power; commit to live true to your self
5. discover your purpose
6. turn your passion into passive/residual profit

7. achieve prosperity through "individual capitalism"
8. practice minimalism
9. uncover your life's limiting deceptions, and break free
10. escape from America (or wherever you feel trapped!)
11. love true to yourself; enjoy global living and dating
12. help others discover/sustain this untethered lifestyle

These steps are based on the realization of a challenge many people face. The solution:

THE INTEGRATED LIFE:

The Challenge: "In the pursuit of economic survival, bodily sustenance and social acceptance, people often (1) disregard their passion in order to focus on a practical career, (2) allow their diet to undermine their health, and (3) deny their sexual and gender wiring in order to conform to societal concepts of relationship. Therein lies the majority of unhappiness in our modern life."

The solution: live the integrated life!

To discover how integrated your life is, and how to make it more so, take the Integrated Life™ test at:

passionprofit.com/integratedlife:

SECTION IV: MORE ▲

APPENDIX [toc]

A Suggested Reading List

A Suggested Viewing List

Open Source Alternatives to Costly Software

Doing Business Abroad (for US taxpayers)

A suggested reading list [appendix]

☐ Read testimonials, travel blogs to raise belief level

☐ BLOG: *Amanda Hocking's kindlepreneur success!*
hockingbooks.com/an-epic-tale-of-how-it-all-happened

☐ ARTICLE: *Darcy Chan kindlepreneur success story*
wsj.com/articles/SB10001424052970204770404577082303350815824

☐ ARTICLE: *Smashwords Author Brian P. earns $100,000 this year*
blog.smashwords.com/2010/12/smashwords-author-brians-pratt-to-earn.html

☐ BOOK: *the Science of Getting Rich* by Wallace Wattles
Passionprofit version available on Amazon

☐ BOOK: *Secrets of the Millionaire Mind*
by T. Harv Eker
Unless you know how to attract and keep it, any money you earn will flow through your hands like air. Understanding your money blueprint is perhaps the most important part of turning your passion into profit.

☐ BOOK: *The E-Myth Revisited: Why Most Small Businesses Don't Work and What to Do About It* by Michael E. Gerber. For an article for Entrepreneur® Magazine, I asked several million- dollar passionpreneurs the secret to success. Almost every person credited this book with helping them think differently about business in general and about their own businesses in particular and made the single most significant impact in their results.

☐ BOOK: *The 22 Immutable Laws of Branding* by Al and Laura Ries *An amazing book I refer to again and again each time I launch a new idea. The principles they present and explain—along with real world examples —are a vital aspect of creating a winning brand for your product or service even as a nomadpreneur.*

☐ BOOK: *No B.S. Marketing to the Affluent* by Dan Kennedy *Sell to the people with money—those who are affected least and last by a recession—and REFUSE to compete with others on price. Compete on uniqueness and value in order to justify your prices.*

A suggested viewing list [appendix]

The movies that inspire me have themes of escape, or unusual or even techie-style rags to riches.

☐ *Shawshank Redemption (1994)*

Persistence against all odds, and freedom!

☐ *Middle Men (2009)*

Somewhat mature theme, based somewhat on actual events; tells the story of two regular guys who stumble upon a business strategy that changed the world as we know it. It has to do with the internet and porn!

☐ *War Dogs (2016)*

Finding business opportunity online. Oh, it also has something to do with illegal gun running.

Oh, and *Scarface (1983)*, of course.

Open source (free) alternatives to commercial (costly) software [appendix]

Open Source Software	Replaces commercial
Open Office LibreOffice	Microsoft Office
GIMP	Adobe Photoshop
Inkscape	Corel Draw Adobe Illustrator
Blender	3Ds Max
OpenShot	iMovie Final Cut

See osalt.com for a comprehensive list of opens source alternatives for all types of software.

Doing business abroad (US citizen taxes) [appendix]

Worldwide tax system – The U.S. taxes its citizens and residents (and domestic corporations) on their worldwide income, from whatever source derived. The

U.S. generally permits a credit (the "foreign tax credit") against U.S. tax for taxes properly paid to other countries on income sourced to such other countries, so long as the effective rate paid to the other country does not exceed the effective rate paid to the

U.S. on that same income. Any excess foreign tax paid becomes a carry forward to future years.

Other countries' tax systems – The tax systems of other countries vary, but most countries have a tax on income similar to the U.S. income tax. To the extent that a U.S. company, citizen or resident conducts business in another country, such foreign country will generally subject the income to its income tax, unless an exception is met or you are protected from that country's income tax under the treaty between the U.S. and the foreign country.

Tax treaties – In order to reduce the risk of duplicate taxation and to encourage international commerce, the U.S. has an income tax treaty with most major countries. A typical treaty provision provides that a U.S. resident or company is not subject to the other country's income tax on income from business conducted in the foreign country, so long as the U.S.

resident or company does not have a "permanent establishment" (which generally means a fixed place of business) in the foreign country. In the case of an individual, the U.S. resident is generally not subject to tax in the foreign country so long as he or she is not present in the country for more than 183 days during the year (unless on the payroll of a foreign company, in which case the salary is typically subject to tax in the foreign country if over a fairly small amount). Other typical treaty provisions provide for a reduced or zero rate of withholding on interest, dividends, rents, royalties and other types of passive income paid by a resident of one country to a resident of the other. [Source: bridgesdunnrankin]

About the Publisher and Author ▲

Walt F.J. Goodridge is from the Caribbean island of Jamaica and holds a Bachelor of Science in Civil Engineering from Columbia University. After seven years working as a civil engineer for the Port Authority of New York & New Jersey, this frustrated employee walked away from his career to pursue his passion for writing and helping others. His mission: *"I share what I know, so that others may grow!"*

In addition to identities as the "Hip Hop Entrepreneur author," "the Jamaican in China," and the "Ageless Adept," Walt is known as the "Passion Prophet," author of *Turn Your Passion Into Profit*, and his unique PassionProfit™ Philosophy & Formula.

Walt escaped from America to the Pacific island of Saipan, Commonwealth of the Northern Mariana Islands (CNMI), and has written several books about his new home: *Saipan Living*, *Doing Business on Saipan*, *Chicken Feathers & Garlic Skin*, S*aipan Now & There's Something About Saipan* and others.

He writes freelance articles for the *Saipan Tribune, Marianas Variety* and *Guam Business Journal;* conducts writer workshops to help aspiring authors; offers tours of the islands; has been featured in books and documentaries about the region; received a Senate Resolution for his contributions to CNMI society; and received *three* Governor's Humanities Awards for (1) Preservation of CNMI History, (2) Research & Publications in the Humanities, and (3) Outstanding Humanities Teacher.

The Wall Street Journal, Entrepreneur Magazine, Source, Billboard, Time, Black Enterprise, Essence, Ebony, South Africa's SArie Magazine as well as "Guerrilla Marketing" guru Jay Conrad Levinson, and music industry pioneer Chuck D, and others have featured, quoted or endorsed his work. His books have been used as texts for university courses in the US and Europe. Walt currently owns and operates over 50 websites, has written well over two dozen books, 400+ business articles and over 500 "life rhymes."

Walt lives an untethered, minimalist, vegan, nomadic lifestyle, but responds to emails to walt@nomadpreneur.com!

Download Walt's CV & Media Kit at www.waltgoodridge.com

Walt enjoys his untethered, minimalist, vegan, nomadic lifestyle on Saipan
Photo: Ferdinand Ramos

Facebook.com/waltgoodridge
Youtube.com/waltgoodridge
Twitter.com/waltgoodridge
and join his "Jamaican in China...and Beyond" adventure at
www.jamaicaninchina.com (blog) and youtube.com/jamaicaninchina

All Walt's Brands

Resources on the following pages may be found at
www.waltgoodridge.com/store

Free Resources for the Nomadpreneur

The Pandemicpreneur Report

How To Make Money in This New Global Paradigm ...Without Ever Leaving Your Home!

A guide for choosing the right product, platform, profit & promotion strategies to generate pandemic-proof income.
- The Pandemicpreneur Toolbox
- 7 business-building strategies
- A Rough & Ready Business Plan
- Links to resources, tools & apps
- Lessons from the past & predictions
- The 23 Laws of Pandemicpreneur Success

The Zero Cost Business Operations Manual

"For every product or service offered at a price on the Internet, there exists a comparable or better alternative offered free!"—Goodridge's Second Law of Internet Economics

Discover all the zero cost (or dirt cheap) resources, tools, services, software and apps I personally use to write and design and publish my books, make videos and courses, create websites, succeed at Search Engine Optimization, run every aspect of daily operation and generate location-free income— for $0 or very close to it!

The Websites That Sell Checklist

To generate income, your website must communicate your value, heighten your credibility, inspire confidence and compel visitors to whip out their credit cards to order your product or service. Online since 1997, I've cracked the code for making sales of "how to" books, biographies, poetry, subscriptions, and even tour guide services for myself and others! Learn the mindset, design process, sales copy style, promotion campaigns and best practices!

Books from the Passionpreneur Series

Books from The Hip Hop Entrepreneur™ Series

Facebook.com/hiphopentrepreneur
Website: www.hiphopentrepreneur.com

The Jamaican Nomad series

Facebook.com/jamaicaninchina
Youtube.com/jamaicaninchina
Blog: www.jamaicaninchina.com

The History We Write™ series

Facebook.com/historywewrite
Website: www.historywewrite.com

Free Resources from the Ageless Adept Series

The Ageless Adept's Master Shopping List, Substitution Checklist & Immunity Top 10

What do I, the Ageless Adept, buy when going grocery shopping? What's in my spice rack? What healthy condiments do I keep on hand? What kind of juicer did I get? Want to see my colloidal silver generator? Yes, I have a coffee grinder (for enemas only, of course!)

Here are the supplements, tools and toys I have on hand at all times--even when I travel--that fit in with the Clean Cell lifestyle and keep me on the path of perfect health, long life and the fountain of youth!

The S.W.E.A.T. Manifesto
The basis of REAL cure—treatment that actually ELIMINATES illness—must & always will require incorporating the power of Sunlight, Water, Earth, Air or Time. (S.W.E.A.T.) This is *The S.W.E.A.T. Manifesto*.

The Sun Cure
The Sun Cure is the re-issue of chapters 38 to 46 of Shelton's Hygienic System Vol II. These chapters from the original text were not included in *Fast & Grow Young*. Shelton explores and explains the numerous physiological, psychological and emotional benefits of direct exposure to sunlight.

REVITALADE™
A mineral REstorative, VITALity-boosting lemonADE!
"The all-natural, great-tasting, made-for-fasting, perfect-for-sauna, microbiome-friendly, energy-enhancing, system-rebooting, mineral-rich, replenisher I developed and have used over the years to live a natural life in an unnatural world!"--The Ageless Adept

Books From the Ageless Adept™ Series

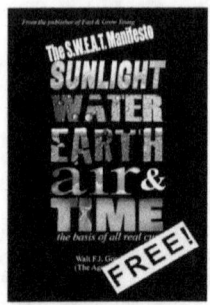
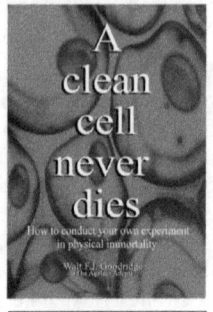

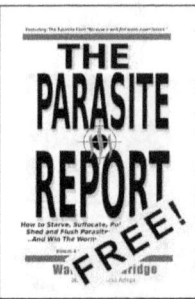

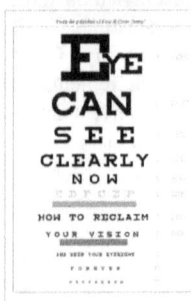

All the Channels & Blogs

The Passion Prophet

"Yes, you CAN turn your passion into profit and earn money doing what you love! Follow my lead!"

Youtube: @therealpassionpreneur
Blog: www.passionpreneur.com/blog

The Ageless Adept™

"How I live a natural life in an unnatural world in my quest for perfect health, long life and the fountain of youth!"

Youtube: @agelessadept
Blog: www.agelessadept.com/blog

The Jamaican on Saipan™

"WWII tours, my daily life, special events, exploration by request & much more on Saipan, Tinian & Rota!"

Youtube: @discoversaipan
Blog: www.discoversaipan.com/blog

The Jamaican in China...and Beyond!

"My adventures throughout the Asia-Pacific region and beyond as a single, nomadic, minimalist, cheapskate!"

Youtube: @jamaicaninchina
Blog: www.jamaicaninchina.com

The Parasite Blog

"A personal journal chronicle of a "parasite fast" as part of a comprehensive protocol to eliminate rope worms.
Blog: www.parasiteblog.com

Tests & Quizzes

What's your Purpose & Passion?
Are you a creator, savior, guru or guide? Take the Purpose-Finder test and discover yourself!
www.passionprofit.com

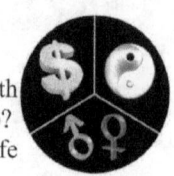

Are you living the Integrated Life?
Are you balancing passion with career, diet with health & sexuality with relationship?
www.passionprofit.com/integratedlife

What's your "Longevity Score?"
How will your dietary and lifestyle choices affect your lifespan? Find out!
www.agelessadept.com/longevity-test

Are you "fit to breed?"
Has Nature classified you as worthy to have your DNA passed on to another generation? Take the test!
www.fittobreed.com

Visit a store called W

Books, apps, audio, video, merchandise, courses, Walt's passion projects, freebies and more from a company called W!
www.waltgoodridge.com/store

www.ingramcontent.com/pod-product-compliance
Lightning Source LLC
Chambersburg PA
CBHW070321190526
45169CB00005B/1690